SKITS THAT TEACH

EDDIE JAMES AND TOMMY WOODARD
THE SKIT GUYS

LACTOSE FREE

FOR THOSE WHO CAN'T STAND CHEESY SKITS

FOREWORD BY WAYNE SLAY—TOMMY AND EDDIE'S YOUTH MINISTER

 ZONDERVAN®

ZONDERVAN.com/
AUTHORTRACKER
follow your favorite authors

Youth Specialties
www.youthspecialties.com

Youth Specialties

Skits That Teach: Lactose-Free for Those Who Can't Stand Cheesy Skits
Copyright © 2006 by Eddie James and Tommy Woodard (The Skit Guys)

Youth Specialties products, 300 South Pierce Street, El Cajon, CA 92020, are published by Zondervan, 5300 Patterson Avenue Southeast, Grand Rapids, MI 49530.

Library of Congress Cataloging-in-Publication Data

James, Eddie, 1970–
  Skits that teach : lactose-free for those who can't stand cheesy skits /
by Eddie James and Tommy Woodard (the skit guys).
      p. cm.
  ISBN-10: 0-310-26569-X (pbk.)
  ISBN-13: 978-0-310-26569-6 (pbk.)
  1. Drama in Christian education. 2. Church group work with teenagers. 3.
Christian drama, American. 4. One-act plays, American. I. Woodard, Tommy.
II. Title.
  BV1534.4.J342 2006
  268'.67—dc22
                                                                                                    2006008471

Web site addresses listed in this book were current at the time of publication. Please contact Youth Specialties via e-mail (YS@Youth-Specialties.com) to report URLs that are no longer operational and provide replacement URLs if available.

Creative Team: Will Penner, Erika Hueneke, Laura Gross, and Heather Haggerty
Cover and Interior Design by SharpSeven

Printed in the United States

07 08 09 10 11 12 • 12 11 10 9 8 7 6 5 4

DEDICATION

To Wayne Slay and Bob Johns

Thanks for seeing more in us than we saw in ourselves.

Our gifts came to light because you took the time to invest.

That investment plays a huge part in all that we are today.

ACKNOWLEDGMENTS

Thanks so much to our wives Angie and Stephanie. We're still amazed you allow us to live the dream.

Thank you: Monty Priest, Jay Howver, Doug Fields, David Rogers, Gary Singleton, and Brian Cates for making us better than we ever thought possible.

Special Thanks to Charissa Fishbeck, Ben Fuqua, Melissa Martinez, Eric Swink, Brian Cropp, Amanda Martin, Ted and Nancie Lowe, Johnny Baker, Andrew Daniels, and Beth McNellan. Your thoughts, ideas, and creativity are such a blessing to us and to everyone who uses this book!

FOREWORD

Okay let's get this over with: it's all my fault! I did it. I was the guy who first asked Tommy and Eddie to do skits in the name of God.

A momentary lapse in judgment? Perhaps. Did I regret it? Sometimes. Lightning in a bottle? You bet!

Here's how it all happened: In 1987, I was serving as a youth pastor in Edmond, Oklahoma, attending a high school variety show as Tommy and Eddie walked on stage to perform a skit. In this skit, Eddie was supposed to be a ventriloquist while Tommy sat on his knee and acted like a dummy. Some things never change.

As a youth pastor, I was always looking for ways to get kids involved in the ministry. As I watched Tommy and Eddie on stage and realized they had connections with our church, I immediately saw an opportunity to enhance the youth ministry at our church. The simple truth was, I could get them involved in ministry, or I could let them sit in the audience and make fun of me while I taught. So I opted to have them use their powers for good instead of evil.

That led to our meeting together every Wednesday night for about an hour before our youth service where I would listen to Tommy and Eddie hash out the topic for the evening and then hold my breath and hope I wouldn't get fired over whatever they came up with. I can't tell you how many times after a skit, I had to correct their theology or political incorrectness.

Twenty years later they're still making people laugh, as well as teaching poignant truths. And they're equipping you to use dramas to get your students laughing and teach biblical principles. You have the same opportunity in your group that I had: you have Skit Guys and Skit Girls just waiting for the opportunity to get involved. The difference is, you now have a resource I didn't have. You have a huge advantage because these skits are tried and proven to make your students laugh and learn in the process.

All Tommy and Eddie needed was an opportunity to explore the gifts God had given them—which is all the Tommys and Eddies in your group need, too. This resource will help them do just that. I hope you will ask God to show you the next Skit Guys or Skit Girls in your group so you'll get to see what I've been able to see God do through the Originals. I wish I'd had this book twenty years ago; no doubt I'd still be using it. I know I would've slept better on Wednesday nights.

May God bless you as you allow God to use this resource to reach kids through drama.

Wayne Slay
Youth pastor of The Skit Guys

TABLE OF CONTENTS

0.0   **INTRODUCTION**   7

1.0   **SKITS FOR IDIOTS**   11
1.1   The Answering Machine   13
1.2   Sin, Spit, and Sight   17
1.3   Caveman   25
1.4   What's Your Story?   27
1.5   Run in Such a Way   32

2.0   **COMEDY**   37
2.1   Adam and Eve   39
2.2   Resist the Devil   44
2.3   Holding Grudges   50
2.4   The Psychic?   54
2.5   The Way We Pray   60

3.0   **DRAMA**   67
3.1   Dirty Rose   69
3.2   Sorry Seems to Be the Hardest Word   72
3.3   The Birdcage   79
3.4   Lost and Found   83
3.5   My Hero   88

4.0   **MONOLOGUES**   93
4.1   Larry the Liar   95
4.2   The Veil   98
4.3   The Big Picture   102
4.4   Welcome Back, Lazarus   105
4.5   Graduation Day   109

5.0   DUETS AND ENSEMBLES   113

DUETS

5.1   Beanie Weenies   115

5.2   Heavenly Daddy   120

5.3   Most Likely To…   124

5.4   Friends Tell Friends Everything   131

5.5   This Year Will Be Different   141

ENSEMBLES

5.6   Piece of a Peace   144

5.7   Sam Goody and the Case of the Selfless Father   149

5.8   Who's Serving Whom?   157

5.9   DTR: Define The Relationship   163

5.10   Here Come the Brides   170

6.0   DRAMATIC READINGS   175

6.1   The Holiness of God   177

6.2   The Life of Christ   180

6.3   Attacking Job   183

6.4   You Wash My Feet, Lord?   186

6.5   The Meaning of Love   188

INTRODUCTION

0.0

"WHAT'S WRONG WITH CHRISTIAN SKITS TODAY?"

It seemed like a simple question—one of those "icebreaker" things you say just to get a discussion started. But when we asked that question at a summer camp in front of about 500 students interested in drama, the response proved to be much more than an icebreaker. It didn't take long to shatter that proverbial ice into a million pieces. In fact, fielding the many answers to our question took up most of the time we had planned for our drama workshop. Here's what some of those teenagers said about Christian skits:

They're cheesy.

They're not written the way we talk; they use words like "groovy" and "totally cool."

The characters start quoting the Bible right away.

They don't feel real.

The Christian character is too perfect.

Christian skits are so mediocre.

It seems like the actors don't spend enough time working on them.

They're sloppy.

They're not funny.

Most of the Christian skits I've seen today are just bad.

They're predictable; you almost always know what's going to happen.

It's the same subjects over and over.

Why does Jesus always have to be sad, mad, or dying?

They really stink.

The actors stand in one place and don't move.

The actors don't connect with the audience.

One person will face the audience, and the others have their backs to the audience.

It seems like some of the actors overact, and others just look uncomfortable on the stage.

It seems like all they talk about is salvation, prayer, love, sex, and dating.

They don't cuss. (Yeah, we didn't get this one either.)

Why were these students saying these things about Christian skits? Was the attitude of this group of kids the byproduct of a hardened, depraved generation?

Nope.

In our "expert" opinion (wow, don't you know it makes our wives proud to say they're married to "skit experts"?), we believe these students were suffering from an overexposure to real entertainment. That's the bottom line. Because even though not every show on television these days can be considered exceptional, the truth is that students get to watch great drama and funny comedy on a daily basis, and those shows become the standard students expect to see. So when they come to church and are subjected to some skit written between the time period of *Laugh-In* and *The Cosby Show*, it's no surprise that they're not impressed or moved.

On top of that, many times those skits are performed by a group of good-hearted people who probably spent more time and effort picking out their socks that morning than they did working on the skit. We're not saying that every performance of your drama group should be Emmy-worthy, but there's a pretty big gap between a sitcom written by a team of comedians and a youth group skit about nose pickin'…for Jesus, of course.

But before you condemn us for our harshness, ask yourself, *How many Christian skits have I watched lately? What kind of impact did they have on the students in the audience?* Unfortunately, many people believe that good skits just *happen*, that you can grab that drama book from 1983 and throw together a totally cool skit that everyone will think is rad. Well, we're here to tell you it ain't as awesome, or as easy, as you may think. And if you've ever had to watch a skit gone wrong, you'll agree with our assessment that most people consider watching a bad skit grody to the max, gnarly, and it makes them wish to be gagged with a spoon.

So we were the ones who did most of the learning at that fateful drama workshop. The answers the students gave us that day provided us with valuable insight into how they perceive Christian skits. They also encouraged us to try our best to make a difference.

"WHAT DO WE DO NOW?"

In our first book, *Instant Skits*, we shared ideas about how to use improv in your student ministry to create memorable moments. We truly believe that if you want fresh, funny, and fabulous skits, your best bet is to have your students create them. But we also know that sometimes your drama team may be as fresh as that unidentifiable goop that's been sitting in a container in the lower back corner of your refrigerator since that Super Bowl outreach party you had in 1995.

That's why we created this book—*Skits That Teach*—because sometimes you need more than an improvisation game. You may be looking for something a little more solid, something to support your message with a message of its own, yet presented with humor that everyone can follow.

In response to what we've learned from different students across the nation, here are the elements we believe are crucial to creating the best skit possible:

1. **CUT THE CHEESE.** We've tried to make sure these skits are suitable for the lactose intolerant. We're actually claiming that these skits are 98 percent cheese-free! However, what we think is cheese-less, you may think is chock-full of cheddar. So, if it's cheesy to you, change it!

2. **NO GROOVY DIALOGUE.** It's not easy for two thirty-something guys to write dialogue that won't eventually become dated. However, we've done our best to avoid phrases, sayings, or clichés that either make you sound totally gnarly or drastically affect your coolness factor. We would also encourage you to make changes to anything that doesn't sound right to you. That way you can keep it real and people will think you're the cat's meow.

3. **DON'T QUOTE ME ON THIS.** Although these scripts contain biblical truth, we promise you will never hear one of our characters say, "The Bible says…" In fact, many times your audience will learn what the Bible says without even knowing that's where it came from.

4. **THE NAMES HAVE BEEN CHANGED TO PROTECT THE INNOCENT.** In an effort to keep our scripts as realistic as possible, we have used many situations that are based on true stories. If anyone asks, we did change the names of the people involved. Oh yeah, and we got their permission to use the stories. (However, for those who did not give us permission, we *still* used their stories *and* their names—just to spite them! You'll find those skits in the "Tell All" chapter of the book.)

5. **FUNNY IS IN THE EYE OF THE BEHOLDER.** Have you ever told a joke that you thought was hilarious, but the person you told it to just smiled, gave you a courtesy laugh, and said, "I don't get it"? We have too, and we hate the way that feels. So hear us when we say that we believe what we've written for you is pretty darn funny. On top of that, most of these skits have already passed inspection—being performed across the nation in front of many different types of audiences—and everyone laughed. Okay, not everyone. But the people who didn't laugh were mean...and unintelligent...and no one really liked them anyway.

6. **HE STINKETH.** There's nothing worse than the response you get when you stink— whether it's because of your crummy performance or the chalupa you ate for lunch. Nobody likes to walk away from a skit and struggle to look people in the eyes as they say things such as: "Hey, you guys are getting better!" or, "Sure looks like you are working real hard at that drama stuff," or, "Wow! That was amazingly horrible. I mean, that sucker really stank it up. I'm thinking you guys just set a new record for the longest stinky skit ever performed!" (Seriously, that last one was something our youth pastor told us when we were younger, and it still sticks with us to this day.) We can't promise that your skits won't stink. What we can promise is that we've done all we can to try to keep them fresh and odor-free. Your job is to make sure your actors are prepared before they get on the stage. No matter how big or small your audience, if a skit is worth doing, it's worth doing to the best of your ability.

7. **I'LL BET YOU DIDN'T SEE THAT COMING.** There's nothing quite like knowing how the story is going to end five lines into the skit. Kinda makes the rest of the skit pointless. We've made a great effort to buck predictability with our skits. Many of them don't have the happy ending where everyone comes to Jesus and pantomimes a Ray Boltz song. Sometimes, you may even see a main character make the wrong decision and suffer for it. Our goal isn't to wrap everything up with a nice bow; we'd rather engage the audience members and let them think for themselves. We want you to hear people say, "I didn't see that coming!"

We've worked really hard to compile a book of solid skits that are relevant, timeless, and useful to your program. We also know that if you look really close, you might find something you don't like or agree with. That's okay; we've done the same thing numerous times with other people's skit books.

So take what we've compiled, change it to fit your audience, and work hard at making it as great as you can make it. If you do those things, we believe you'll be a success in the world of skitology. Most of all, have fun and do your best.

—Eddie and Tommy (a.k.a., The Skit Guys)

SKITS FOR IDIOTS

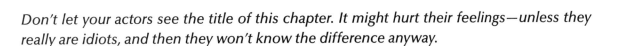

1.0

Don't let your actors see the title of this chapter. It might hurt their feelings—unless they really are idiots, and then they won't know the difference anyway.

Maybe you have a group of students who are just beginning to use drama. Maybe you've waited until the last minute to put together your skit and you need something fast. Maybe your associate pastor and education minister are looking to break into drama. In all these situations, "Skits for Idiots" is your answer.

These skits have good messages and are easy to put together. Each skit has a minimum number of prop requirements and simple staging. In most cases there are very few lines to memorize; in some cases the actors can actually use scripts during the performance. We weren't kidding when we said they were written for idiots!

SKIT TIPS

Just because these are simple skits, that doesn't mean you don't have to put forth a little effort. Here are some ideas to keep in mind as you prepare to use "Skits for Idiots":

1. **READ THROUGH THE SCRIPT IN ADVANCE.** This will help you secure the actors you'll need to play each role and give you time to pull together the props you'll need.

2. **CHOOSE ACTORS WHO CAN IMPROV.** With any performance there is a possibility for mistakes, so the actors need to be able to "roll with the punches." This possibility is intensified with a skit that's thrown together just a few minutes before the performance. So just be sure your "idiots" are flexible!

3. **MAKE EACH SCRIPT YOUR OWN.** To make it easier for your actors, make all of your desired changes to the script *before* giving it to them. Feel free to cut things out or rewrite things so the skits are easier for your actors. Also, remember that by changing just a few words in some of the scripts, you can make those skits work with almost any message.

4. **HAVE FUN!** Above all else, have a great time with these scripts. Use them as tools to praise your drama team. Let the audience know you gave the actors the script just 30 minutes before performance time, and they'll appear to be master thespians! And then we'll have to change the name of this chapter!

"THE ANSWERING MACHINE"

BY EDDIE JAMES & TOMMY WOODARD WITH THE SKITIOTS

WHAT: It's Glenn's birthday, and he must deal with the "well-wishers" who have left him messages. (Themes: identity in Christ, parents, rejection, disappointment)

WHO: Glenn, Stevie, Dad, Ex-Girlfriend, Grandma, Mom

WHERE: Glenn's house

WHEN: Present day

WHY: Deuteronomy 31:8; Matthew 18:10-14; Philippians 2:3

WEAR:
(COSTUMES AND PROPS) Answering machine, cell phone, backpack, stand for answering machine, couch or some added furniture (allows audience to be brought into the scene better), sound effects for answering machine beep, current love song

HOW: Because of the timing issues of the offstage (or prerecorded) voices, it's very important that Glenn reacts to what is being said through the machine. Make sure this has been worked out beforehand with the answering machine beep. The sound could come from a "telephone toy" put up to a microphone backstage.

Glenn enters carrying a backpack, talking on his cell phone.

Glenn: Yeah, Dad, yeah, I got the tickets. I can't believe you got me tickets to the game for my birthday…Yeah, I'll be ready when you get here…Check the messages? Sure. See you when you get here…I love you, too. (To answering machine) Let's see who remembered my birthday.

Glenn pushes "Play" button on the machine. Note: These messages should either be voiced through an offstage microphone or prerecorded.

Stevie: Yo, yo, yo. What's up? What's up? This is your pal Stevie wanting to wish his peep a hizzy on the b-day! Catch you later, man.

Answering machine beeps.

Stevie: Uh, this is Stevie again. I just wanted to make sure you knew that when I wished you a hizzy on the b-day I meant happy birthday. But you probably already knew that. Just checking. Bye.

Answering machine beeps.

Ex-Girlfriend: Hey you...It's Misty. Um, I just wanted to call you up on your special day. Last year it was *our* special day. Remember, I made you dinner...and I burned dinner...and I burned you. I hope your eyebrows have grown back! I know we only went out for a week, but it was the best week of my life. Anyway, I know I'm not supposed to talk to you, but I decided to make you a cake, and...oh my, do you hear that? (*Audience can hear song in background.*) It's our song! (*She begins singing a few phrases of a current love ballad—badly, and nearly sobbing.*) I can't take this anymore! I'm sorry. I know I'm not allowed within 500 feet of your house, so I guess I'll just eat the cake I made for you and watch (*insert some romantic movie name here*). (*Very quick change of tone to sounding sinister*) But Glenn, I hope you know that nothing can keep us apart. Not even that restraining order. Buh-bye!

Answering machine beeps.

Grandma: Honey? Happy birthday from your Mee Maw and Pee Paw. (*Insert age here*) years! I remember it like it was yesterday. We got there about three hours after your mother had gone into labor. When you finally popped out, you were so pretty. Your Pee Paw said you looked like a dried prune, and he tried to eat you. But you know his cataracts. (*She gets choked up.*) I promised myself I wouldn't cry this year. Well, anyway, here's your birthday blessing: (*Begins singing*) Happy birthday to...

Glenn hits the button on the machine and it beeps.

Answering machine beeps.

Mom: Hey, it's Mom. (***Glenn*** *sits down*) Um, this weekend...I know, I know, I know this is our weekend, but something's come up. I have to go to Chicago. I'm really sorry, but I have to go. Don't make that face. I know you're making that face. This is important. I need to go so I can get that promotion. I promise I'll make it up to you. We'll go on a big shopping spree when I get back. (*Short pause*) Or I can just give you some money. (*Then rushing*) Whatever you prefer. You'll just have to spend another week at your dad's. Uh oh, that's my flight. Look, we'll sort it all out when I get back. I gotta go. Bye.

Glenn hits the button on machine and it beeps.

Glenn: (*To himself*) I can't believe she forgot her own son's birthday.

Glenn starts to pick up the phone and *Dad* enters.

Dad: Hey, Glenn, you ready? Did you check the messages?

Glenn: Yeah.

Dad: Anything for me?

Glenn: Mom called.

Dad: To wish you a…

Glenn: Mom can't take me this weekend.

Dad: She forgot your birthday again? (*From* **Glenn's** *reaction*) I'm sorry.

Glenn: I just…I just wanna know…What it is about me that's not worth it to her?

Dad: (*Pause*) Glenn. Listen. I know things aren't the way they should be, but she's still your mother, and you need to respect her. Besides, you can't live your life based on what other people think of you. (*Pause*) You are *worth* it. You're worth it to me, you're worth it to God, and I know that somewhere deep down you're worth it to your mom. What you need to realize, even though it's a hard realization, is that people just can't give what they don't have. Showing affection has always been hard for your mom. (*Pause*) Maybe she'll call back.

Glenn: Forget it. Let's just go.

Dad: You're sure?

Glenn: Yeah.

They start to leave. The phone starts to ring. They turn and look at the phone.

Dad: Hey, you wanna get that? It could be your mom.

Glenn: Nah. C'mon, let's go.

They leave. Answering machine picks up.

THE END.

"SIN, SPIT, AND SIGHT"
BY TOMMY WOODARD & EDDIE JAMES WITH ERIC SWINK

WHAT: This skit is a fun, interactive way to read through the biblical passage of one of Jesus' greatest miracles—the healing of a blind man. (Themes: healing, salvation, power of Christ)

WHO: Reader, Blind Man, Jesus, Disciples (two to 12), Neighbor 1, Neighbor 2

WHERE: A busy street corner

WHEN: Biblical times

WHY: Psalm 30:2; Luke 6:19; John 9:1-12

WEAR: Bible
(COSTUMES AND PROPS)

HOW: A note about casting: Reader should be played by whoever is going to be doing the teaching during this session. You can use from two to 12 disciples. Also, please don't feel like you need to do everything written in the script. Use what works and toss what doesn't. The reader needs to keep in mind that if one of the other actors forgets to do something, that's okay—just keep reading.

---

*The skit begins with **Reader** speaking to the audience. The **Reader** has a Bible with the script in it so the Scripture passage is easily readable.*

Reader: Today, I've asked our drama team to help me with the message by acting out a passage as I read it. They're going to show you what this particular event might have looked like. I'll be reading from John chapter nine. (*Opens Bible and begins to read*) As he, Jesus, went along...(***Jesus** and **Disciples** enter*) he saw a man blind from birth. (***Blind Man** enters from the opposite side pretending to walk with a seeing-eye dog*) Um...what are you doing?

Blind Man:	I'm walking.
Reader:	No, I mean, why is your arm sticking out like that?
Blind Man:	Oh, that's my seeing-eye dog. Pretty good, huh?
Reader:	Yeah, not bad, but they didn't have seeing-eye dogs during biblical times.
Blind Man:	Oh, I didn't realize this was during biblical times.
Reader:	It *is* from the Bible, you know.
Blind Man:	Yeah, I just thought...(*Can't come up with anything*) Let's try that again. (*Exits stage*)
Reader:	Okay, let's just start all over. (*Motions for **Jesus** and **Disciples** to exit stage as well*) As he, Jesus, went along...(***Jesus** and **Disciples** enter*) he saw a man blind from birth.

Blind Man enters from the opposite side with arm extended as if he is being led by something much bigger than a dog.

Reader:	Okay, now what are you doing?
Blind Man:	Well, I thought that since they didn't have seeing-eye dogs during biblical times, I'd have a seeing-eye camel! Pretty cool, huh? It's like you can almost *see* the camel standing there!
Reader:	Okay, look, they didn't have seeing-eye dogs or seeing-eye camels.
Blind Man:	Oxen?

As ***Blind Man*** mentions each animal, *he* moves his arm up or down, demonstrating where each animal's leash would be.

Reader:	No.
Blind Man:	Goats?
Reader:	No!

Blind Man:	Llamas?
Reader:	NO! Look, why don't you just sit down where you are.
Blind Man:	Well, how'd I get here?
Reader:	I don't know. (*Looks at Bible*) The Bible doesn't say. It just says he was there.
Blind Man:	Are you sure they didn't have seeing-eye camels? (*Raises arm back up to camel height*)
Reader:	Sit!
Blind Man:	Okay…okay.
Reader:	(*Goes back to reading*) His disciples asked him, "Rabbi, who sinned, this man or his parents, that he was born blind?" (**Disciples** *just stand there silently*) Hey, guys, that's your cue.
Jesus:	Yeah, they don't know which one is supposed to say it.
Reader:	It doesn't say; it just says, "His disciples asked him…"
Jesus:	So…how do they know who's supposed to say it?
Reader:	Look, it doesn't matter. Just say it.

Disciples all begin to speak at once, talking over each other and making it impossible to understand them. After realizing how confusing it is, they huddle together for a moment, and then stand back in their places.

Jesus:	Okay, let's try that again.
Reader:	His disciples asked him, "Rabbi, who sinned, this man or his parents, that he was born blind?"

Disciples say the line "Rabbi, who…" with each person saying one word right after the other.

Reader: (*Looks at audience and rolls eyes*) "Neither this man nor his parents sinned," said Jesus, "but this happened so that the work of God might be displayed in his life. As long as it is day, we must do the work of him who sent me. Night is coming, when no one can work. While I am in the world, I am the light of the world."

Jesus: I say what?

Reader: "Neither this man nor his parents sinned," said Jesus, "but this happened so that the work of God might be displayed in his life. As long as it is day, we must do the work of him who sent me. Night is coming, when no one can work. While I am in the world, I am the light of the world."

Jesus: Neither this man nor his parents sinned. This happened at night so he could work a light display for God…the world…I am…something, something, something…whatever else you said. (***Reader*** *looks at* ***Jesus***, *frustrated*) What? That is a bunch of lines. Come on. At least I didn't make up a seeing-eye camel!

Blind Man: Hey, that's not very Christ-like.

Reader: Okay, that's enough. Let's keep going. Having said this, he spit on the ground…

Jesus: (*Looking at* ***Reader***) You want me to what?

Reader: Spit.

Jesus: Come on, do you really think the Son of God would do that?

Reader: Yes.

Jesus: Why?

Reader: (*Pointing at the Bible*) Because it's in here.

Jesus: Oh yeah. (*Begins to hock up a big loogy*)

Reader: (*Disgusted*) Now, I don't think he would do that.

Jesus: Sorry. (*Thinks for a moment*) Let there be spit.

Reader:	Would you just spit?!
Jesus:	Okay! (*Pretends to spit*)
Reader:	And he made some mud with the saliva (***Jesus*** *pretends to make mud*), and put it on the man's eyes.
Blind Man:	(*Jumps up*) No way! That's sick.
Reader:	Come on.
Blind Man:	No way! *You* let him put spit-mud on your eyes!
Reader:	Look, the guy wanted to see. He didn't care if Jesus put mud on his eyes or not.
Blind Man:	Fine. (***Jesus*** *pantomimes putting mud on* ***Blind Man's*** *eyes*) This is gross! This is so not a "spa treatment."
Reader:	(*Reads*) "Go," he told him, "wash in the Pool of Siloam."
Jesus:	Go wash in the Pool of Salami.
Reader:	So the man went and washed. (***Blind Man*** *stands up and begins to walk with pretend seeing-eye camel*) Hey, what did I tell you about the seeing-eye camel?
Blind Man:	Hey, look, I've got spit-mud on my eyes. If I have to walk around with spit-mud on my eyes, at least give me the dignity of a seeing-eye camel. Besides, I don't know where the pool is, but the camel does.
Reader:	Okay, whatever. Just go wash.
Blind Man:	Believe me, I can't wait. (***Blind Man*** *pretends to kneel down and wash*)
Reader:	So the man went and washed, and came home seeing. (***Blind Man*** *looks sad and pantomimes hugging his camel*) What are you doing?
Blind Man:	I'm saying goodbye to Sally.
Reader:	Sally?

Blind Man:	My seeing-eye camel. Can I please have a little privacy here?
Reader:	Just go home seeing!
Blind Man:	Okay! (*Looks offstage and says in a quiet voice*) Goodbye, old friend; I'll miss you. (*Starts to sing popular love song of heartache and loss*)
Reader:	Will you go already?!

*He walks off and is met by the **Neighbors**.*

Reader:	His neighbors, and those who had formerly seen him begging, asked, "Isn't this the same man who used to sit and beg?" Some claimed that he was. Others said, "No, he only looks like him." But he himself insisted, "I am the man."
Neighbor 1:	Isn't this the same man who used to sit and beg?
Blind Man:	I'm da man...Yo, yo what's up my peeps? (*Or current slangy greeting*)
Neighbor 2:	No, he only looks like him.
Blind Man:	I'm da man.
Neighbor 1:	You can't be him. You're not blind.
Blind Man:	I'm da man.
Neighbor 2:	Yeah, you only look like him.
Blind Man:	I'm da man.
Neighbors:	Nuh uh.
Blind Man:	Uh huh.
Neighbors:	Nuh uh.
Blind Man:	Uh huh.
Neighbors:	Nuh uh.

Blind Man:	Uh huh.
Neighbors:	Nuh uh.
Blind Man:	Uh huh.
Neighbor 1:	Oh yeah? Then where's your camel?
Reader:	Enough! Can we get back to the Bible, please? (***Blind Man*** and ***Neighbors*** *apologize*) "How then were your eyes opened?" they demanded.
Neighbor 2:	Tell us how your eyes were opened, or we'll shoot you!
Reader:	What are you doing?
Neighbor 1:	We're making our demand!
Reader:	(*Rolls eyes and looks at audience as if to say, "What a bunch of idiots!"*) I don't think that's what it means.
Neighbor 1:	You can't prove it!
Reader:	Okay, let's just get on with it. (*Reads*) He replied, "The man they call Jesus made some mud and put it on my eyes. He told me to go to Siloam and wash. So I went and washed, and then I could see."
Blind Man:	Don't shoot! I'll tell you whatever you want to know. The truth is—I'm a spy!
Reader:	Would you just repeat after me?! Please!
Blind Man:	Okay! (*Monotone voice*) The man they call Jesus made some spit-mud and put it on my eyes. He told me to go to Siloam and wash. So I went and washed, and then I could see.
Neighbor 1:	That's gross. You let him put spit-mud on your face? That's disgusting! You're gross.
Blind Man:	(*Pointing at **Reader***) He made me do it! He also hated my seeing-eye camel.
Reader:	Okay, okay...let's move on. (*Reads*) "Where is this man?" they asked him.

Neighbor 2:	We knew you were a spy! Now, where is this man you speak of?
Reader:	(*Realizing he has lost control*) "I don't know," he said.
Blind Man:	You'll never get it out of me!
Neighbor 1:	We have ways of making you talk.
Blind Man:	Okay, okay. Look, I don't know where Jesus is right now. All I know is, I was blind, but now I see.
Neighbor 2:	That's amazing. You ought to make that into a song.
Neighbor 1:	Yeah. Hey, I'll tell you what—come over to my house, and we'll pick something out on the piano.

(*The three exit*)

Reader:	(*To audience*) You know, I don't think that's exactly the way it happened. But that's not the point. The point is the guy was blind, he encountered Jesus, and then he could see. And you know what? Jesus wants to have an encounter with you that will change you forever. But be careful—he may ask you to get messy, to go someplace special, and to wash up. But trust me, it will all be worth it.

*At this point, the **Reader** may want to encourage those in the audience to take some time to reflect on what God may be doing in their lives right now. If the setting would lend itself to people sharing about times when they had to "get messy for God," that would be very appropriate and effective. If the setting is not conducive to sharing, have a testimony planned to help people see what it means to "get messy for God" today.*

THE END.

"CAVEMAN"

BY EDDIE JAMES & TOMMY WOODARD WITH ANDREW DANIELS

WHAT: In this silent skit a caveman does everything he can to catch the eye of a cave-woman. (Themes: men and women, dating, love, fun)

WHO: Caveman, Cavewoman

WHEN: Prehistoric times

WHY: Genesis 2:18-24; Proverbs 18:22; Ephesians 5

WEAR: Caveman attire. Additional props: caveman club (big Wiffle™ ball bat wrapped
(COSTUMES   with brown packing tape), and a red rose placed on the ground opposite from
AND PROPS)   where Cavewoman stands

HOW: There aren't any "real" lines in this script. For the most part, it's really an im-
promptu scene between two characters. The script is a basic scenario, but feel
free to add to this scene as you see fit. Most of the humor is derived as the
actors "grunt" based on their characters' emotional response to the other's
actions.

Another idea would be to add music in the background during certain sec-
tions. For instance, "Twisted Nerve" by Bernard Herrmann (otherwise known
as the "Woohoo" song in a bunch of Vonage commercials) would work well
in the beginning. Then when the caveman comes back with the rose, add in a
current love song. Get as creative as possible with this one.

Caveman enters. *Cavewoman is standing center stage.* *Caveman "struts" by her and glances over
his shoulder to see if she's looking, but she pays him no attention. He crosses in front of her again
and receives the same response.*

*Caveman walks up to Cavewoman and "checks her out," grunting with approval. Cavewoman
turns her back, grunting in a "what do you think you're looking at?" manner.*

Caveman walks to where *Cavewoman* can see him and starts posing and flexing like a body-builder (instead of straight flexing, the *Caveman* should look like he's doing some type of activity—such as stretching—and "accidentally" ends in a muscle-man pose). *Cavewoman* turns again and grunts as if she isn't impressed.

Caveman walks past *Cavewoman* and trips and falls, acting as though he's injured. *Cavewoman* is still not moved.

Caveman walks over to *Cavewoman* and stands beside her. He slowly does the trying-to-be-cool-arm-around-the-shoulders thing. *Cavewoman* makes eye contact with *Caveman* and removes his arm from her shoulders.

Caveman starts to storm off. But before he exits, he notices a rose lying on the ground. He picks it up and smiles at the audience, as if an idea has just crossed his mind. He slowly walks over to *Cavewoman* (with the rose behind his back), pulls the rose out, and presents it to her as a gift. *Cavewoman* responds with happiness and excitement. She looks up at *Caveman*, smiling. *Caveman* takes his club, hits her on the head with it—knocking her out—puts her over his shoulder, and carries her offstage, grunting with approval.

THE END.

"WHAT'S YOUR STORY?"
BY EDDIE JAMES & TOMMY WOODARD WITH THE SKITIOTS

WHAT: Everyone has a story about what God is doing in and around them. But sometimes a lack of attention or a need to compare ourselves to others can cause us to miss what God really wants us to share. (Themes: testimony, guilt, comparison, sharing)

WHO: Teacher, Mike, Ashley

WHEN: Present day

WHY: Psalm 40:5; Isaiah 43:19; 1 Peter 3:15

WEAR:
(COSTUMES
AND PROPS) None

HOW: This skit can be performed two ways:

1. Plant two actors in the audience for the teacher to interact with, or,

2. Have all the characters up on the stage and the two students sitting on chairs.

If you choose to do it the first way, the person playing the teacher can address everyone in the audience along with the two actors. Mike and Ashley should stand up when they say their lines.

Feel free to change the song title, TV show, and evangelistic crusade to stay current, if need be.

Teacher addresses the audience.

Teacher: Today I'm here to ask you all to tell your stories. Everyone has a story of what God is doing or has done in her life. So if anyone would be willing to share, I'd love to hear your testimony about what God has been doing. (**Mike** raises hand) You over there, what's your story?

Mike:	Well, yeah, I'm in this band, and we're getting pretty big, you know. I mean, God is doing really big things.
Teacher:	Great.
Mike:	Yeah, it really is. I mean, we have this one big hit—I'm sure everyone here has heard it. It goes like this…(*Mike begins singing any popular song, such as Switchfoot's "Meant to Live," and then says to the people around him*) Come on, sing with me…
Teacher:	Wait. You're not in Switchfoot…That's a Switchfoot song…
Mike:	Umm, yeah, I know, but I have their CD…
Teacher:	I don't think you understood my question. Have a seat. Okay, the question was, what is *your* story? What is God doing in *your* life? (*Ashley raises her hand*) Yes, you over there.
Ashley:	I'm actually going through a really hard time right now, and I could use a lot of prayer. See, recently my friends and I all split up and went our separate ways.
Teacher:	Wow, that's hard.
Ashley:	Yeah, it has been. We always had these crazy experiences, and we always met in this little coffee shop called Central Perk. I mean, there was me, Joey, Chandler, Monica…
Teacher:	Wait. You're talking about the TV show *Friends*. That's a sitcom.
Ashley:	No, that's not true. We would meet every Thursday at seven o'clock for a half hour.
Teacher:	Never mind. Have a seat. All right, I don't think I'm making myself clear. What is God doing in *your* life? (*Mike raises his hand again*) Yes, you again.
Mike:	Yeah, I didn't understand the first time, but I get it now.
Teacher:	Okay, good. Go ahead.

Mike:	Yeah, the other day God put a huge task in front of me. I mean, this fellowship of believers and I had to basically save the world. We had this ring, and we had to destroy it in the mountain of Mordor. We had an elf with us, and there were dragons. I had really hairy feet at the time…
Teacher:	All right, you can't talk anymore. That's *The Lord of the Rings*. Please, anyone, tell me what God is doing in *your* life.
Ashley:	God has been doing big things in my ministry. I mean, all these crazy things have been happening.
Teacher:	Okay, like what?
Ashley:	Well, we have these huge revivals where tons of people come to hear about Christ, and just a lot of people get saved, and it's just amazing.
Teacher:	What's your ministry called?
Ashley:	Oh, it's the, um, Ashley Graham Crusades. Yeah, that's it.
Teacher:	You mean the *Billy* Graham Crusades? That's not you. Have a seat. All right, I don't see why this is so difficult. This is ridiculous. Please, will anyone tell me something God has done in *your* life? (**Mike** *raises his hand;* **Teacher** *ignores him*) Anyone? Please, anyone at all? Anyone but Mike. Please, please let there be someone other than Mike. (*After a pause when no one else raises a hand*) Okay, Mike, go ahead.
Mike:	Yes! Sorry about before. I didn't know you meant what God is doing in *my* life! I got it now. Sorry about that.
Teacher:	Right, just go ahead.
Mike:	Well, I actually just got back from a mission trip in Brazil.
Teacher:	Oh, wow! (*Starts flipping through his notes*)
Mike:	Yeah, it was awesome! I mean, God did big things there. A lot of people made professions of faith in Jesus. God moved in mighty, mighty ways.
Teacher:	Wait, it says here in my records that you've never left the country.

Mike: Right. I meant Brazil…Alabama. Yeah, it was so great in Brazil, Alabama. The people were…

Teacher: Stop it!

Mike: But I was used by God to reach these Brazilian/Alabamians to…

Teacher: No, you weren't.

Mike: (*Pause for a moment*) But you could imagine if I did…

Teacher: Please sit. All right. Please, for the love of all that is holy, do any of you have a story of your own? A personal testimony of what God has done in your life? (**Ashley** *raises hand, so* **Teacher,** *exasperated, says*) I don't even care anymore. Sure, what is it?

Ashley: Well, when you said "testimony," it sparked a memory of an experience of mine. When I was in seventh grade, I went to church camp, and it was awesome. We got to help and serve a lot of people there. God really did a lot of things that summer.

Teacher: That's exactly what I was looking for. So you went to church camp when you were in seventh grade, and God did awesome things there? That's really cool. So since you've shared a little bit, what else has God done in your life?

Ashley: What do you mean?

Teacher: Well, how old are you now?

Ashley: I'm a senior.

Teacher: Right. God did awesome things that year in seventh grade, so what else has God done in your life since then? How else have you grown?

Ashley: Well, I go to church camp every year…

Teacher: Is that all that's happened? You had an awesome experience a few years ago, and you haven't seen God move since then?

Ashley: Um…not really. Maybe I don't understand the question.

Teacher: Okay, you can have a seat. Thanks for sharing. Look, it's so easy for us to get caught in this trap of living through the experiences of others and the experiences we had in the past. So here's the question: What does God want to do with you? If someone asks for your story, what will you tell them?

Mike: (*Brief pause*) Well, I'd tell them about the time I healed a man who was unable to walk. I reached out and...

Teacher: Mike! This meeting is over. Go out and create some experiences of your own. Let God actually use you to do something.

THE END.

"RUN IN SUCH A WAY"
BY TOMMY WOODARD & EDDIE JAMES

WHAT: Appearances aside, there's a difference between "talking the talk" and "walking the walk"—or as this skit demonstrates, running the race. (Themes: disciplined living, hypocrites)

WHO: Non-Runner, Starter, Runners (*Optional:* Non-Runner's Helper)

WHERE: Starting line of a race

WHEN: Present day

WHY: 1 Corinthians 9:24; Philippians 3:12-14; James 1:22

WEAR:
(COSTUMES AND PROPS)
Runners should be dressed in normal running attire. Starter can dress casually and will need a starter's pistol. The Non-Runner should be dressed in the most extravagant running outfit you can find and carrying a backpack or duffle bag of some kind containing: a boom box, a good-sized snack cake, a can of soda, and a pack of cigarettes

HOW: This is a silly skit with a powerful conclusion. It would be good to create an aisle in the middle of the audience for the Runners to run down.

---

*First onstage are the **Runners**, stretching and preparing for the race just to the right of center stage. The **Starter** enters and takes her place just left of center stage.*

Starter: Runners to your mark…(***Runners*** *move into a straight line facing the audience*) Get set…(***Runners*** *get into starting stance, and **Starter** raises pistol over her head*)

Non-Runner: (*Enters with bag in hand*) Wait! Don't start yet. Just a minute!

Starter *and **Runners** react with confusion, looking a little startled and waiting to see what the **Non-Runner** does.*

OPTION: *If you have an extra person, you may want to use him or her here as the "**Non-Runner's Helper**." This character would carry all the **Non-Runner's** gear, and at this point in the skit, the **Helper** would run in and stop the race for the **Non-Runner**. Throughout the skit, this character assists the **Non-Runner** by handing him whatever he needs and behaving as though the **Non-Runner** is the greatest gift to the sport ever. Caution: Be careful not to let this character overpower the **Non-Runner**.*

Non-Runner:	Sorry I'm late. Give me just a minute and we'll get this party started! (*Takes off any warm-up gear to reveal his extravagant running outfit, and then looks at the other runners and addresses them*) Like the way this looks? (*Gestures to the front of his outfit*) Well, take a good look, 'cause all you're gonna be seeing is this! (*Gestures to his backside. Addresses the **Starter**) Okay...let's do this thing!
Starter:	Runners to your mark...(***Runners** move into a straight line facing the audience*) Get set...(***Runners** get into starting stance, and **Starter** raises pistol*)
Non-Runner:	Hold it! Hold it! Whoa! I almost forgot to stretch and warm up. Hang on one second, fellas. (*Reaches into bag and takes out "boom box." Sets it down, pushes "play." While a short portion of "Let's Hear It for the Boy," "Eye of the Tiger," or something similar is playing, the **Non-Runner** does what he thinks is the coolest workout, but in actuality looks ridiculous. After he has finished "warming up," he turns to the **Runners** and says*) Okay, losers, LET'S DO IT! (*Addressing the **Starter**) All right "Big'un"...hit it.
Starter:	Runners to your mark...(***Runners** form a line*) Get set...(***Runners** get into starting stance, and **Starter** raises pistol*)
Non-Runner:	Wait a minute. Wait...A...Minute! Oh my! I cannot believe I was about to run on an empty stomach. (*Reaches in his bag and pulls out a good-sized snack cake. Opening it, he looks at the other runners and says*) Breakfast-O-Champions. (*Shoves the entire cake into his mouth, eating it as fast as he can. While chewing the cake, the **Non-Runner** taunts the other runners, telling them what losers they are and how badly he's going to beat them. Finishing the snack cake, he turns again to the **Starter** and says*) Well, are we going to start this thing or not?
Starter:	Runners to your mark...(***Runners** form a line*) Get set...(***Runners** get into starting stance, and **Starter** raises pistol*)

Non-Runner: (*Stands up, holds up one finger, and says to the* ***Starter***) Hold on ONE minute. (*Looks at the other runners and says*) Now I'm kinda thirsty. (*Goes back to bag, pulls out a soda, pops the top, and downs the whole thing in one giant gulp. If possible, he looks at the* ***Runners*** *and burps out, "Losers!" Once ready, he looks at the other* ***Runners*** *and says*) You better get ready, 'cause like the broom said to the vacuum, "You're about to eat my dust!" (***Runners*** *look at each other with confusion.* ***Non-runner*** *turns to* ***Starter*** *in frustration and says*) Hello? Today? Please?

Starter: Runners to your mark...(***Runners*** *form a line*) Get set...(***Runners*** *get into starting stance, and* ***Starter*** *raises pistol*)

Non-Runner: Oh my! What am I thinking? I can't believe I almost ran without one of these little guys! (*Reaches in bag and pulls out a cigarette. If it won't put your job in jeopardy, have the* ***Non-Runner*** *"light up" and pretend to smoke. He offers cigarettes to the other* ***Runners***, *who refuse. Finishing his smoke, he looks at the other* ***Runners*** *and says*) Oh yeah...talk about my second wind! That was just what I needed. And now, get ready, 'cause I'm gonna smoke *you* next!

Starter: (*Obviously frustrated*) Runners to your mark...(***Runners*** *form a line*) Get set...(***Runners*** *get into starting stance, and* ***Starter*** *raises pistol*)

When the ***Starter*** *fires the pistol, all the* ***Runners*** *sprint off the stage—through the audience, if possible. The* ***Non-Runner*** *simply stands up, watches them run off, and turns to start packing up his stuff.*

Starter: (*Looking confused, says to the* ***Non-Runner***) I fired the starting pistol.

Non-Runner: Pardon me?

Starter: I said, I fired the starting pistol. Didn't you hear it?

Non-Runner: Oh yeah, I heard it.

Starter: Well?

Non-Runner: (*Pauses for a moment, trying to figure out what the* ***Starter*** *wants*) Oh...sorry... uh, you did a fine job of starting the race. I mean, really, the authoritative voice, nice posture, and the gun...well, that just sent it over the top!

Starter: No! That's not what I mean. Look, are you going to run this race or not?

Non-Runner: Me? (*Laughing*) No. Of course not! Come on...run? That's a good one! I don't actually run. I just come here to look good. (*As he walks off he says*) Me run—that's rich! Like I'd be that interested in a race. (*Brief pause*) So, see you next week?

Lights fade out, if possible. If not, have **Non-Runner** *take his gear offstage.* **Starter** *shrugs her shoulders and also walks off.*

OPTION: PowerPoint slide: "Do you not know that in a race all the runners run, but only one gets the prize? Run in such a way as to get the prize." (1 Corinthians 9:24)

THE END.

COMEDY 2.0

SHOW ME THE FUNNY!

Comedy is like a family reunion—when it's good, everyone has fun together. But when it's bad, you have to eat unidentifiable casseroles, listen to stories about your relatives' strange surgeries, and kiss that aunt with the hair-covered mole on her lip.

In our minds, there really is nothing more painful than watching bad comedy. Okay, actually *performing* bad comedy does hurt worse. Whatever side of the stage you're on, the idea is to avoid bad comedy at all costs. The thing is, comedy is a tough subject because it's so subjective. Many times comedy is about making fun of some part of life or just looking at it from a slanted perspective. Therefore, what one person finds funny, another may find offensive.

There are also different levels of comedy. *Low comedy* includes those questionable subjects like bodily functions and funny sounds. We call that "potty humor." It's called "low comedy" because pretty much everyone can understand it (though whether or not they laugh at it is an entirely different matter). On the other end, you have *high comedy*, which includes satire and humorous commentary. Some people will miss some of the humor because either they don't have the prerequisite knowledge that allows them to see the connections, or they simply don't want to think that hard. We call that "the stuff that kept *Frasier* on the air for 10 years."

Typically, comedy stretches reality a little bit out of proportion. Tiny details or behaviors are emphasized and taken out of context, enabling us to see how many things we do and say that make little sense or are completely ridiculous. Comedy focuses on the absurdity that is at the core of so much that we do; and because we cannot rationalize something that doesn't make sense, we have to laugh at it.

Comedy breaks down walls; it helps people lower their defenses; and it opens up doors to people's minds. Used effectively in Christian skits, comedy becomes a wonderful precursor to introducing the truth. Comedy, like any tool, can be used to build up or to tear down. We encourage you to use your comedic powers for good.

SKIT TIPS

1. **CHOOSE "THE OTHER WHITE MEAT."** With comedy, you want to pick the "hams" from your group. As we stated in our previous book, *Instant Skits* (shameless plug!), improv or a comedic script is best handled by the people who can make you laugh "offstage." These people are naturally the center of attention, and they don't mind taking risks. So they're the ones you want working your comedy. The truth is, people who don't know how to time a joke or wait for a laugh won't be successful at comedy—no matter how hard they try. So think of three-to-five funny people in your group—guys and girls—and ask them to join you. Truth is, they're either going to make people laugh from the stage or out in the audience while you're trying to teach. We suggest you harness their power and use it for your good, or else they may use it against you. Why do you think our youth pastor finally asked *us* to be in skits?

2. **TASTE THIS AND TELL ME IF IT'S OKAY.** Aunt Nelda didn't cook using a recipe; she tasted whatever she was making and had other people taste it before she pronounced it "ready." Comedy works the same way. Before you put your actors onstage, watch the skit. Have others watch it too. Did you laugh? Are the others laughing? If not, can you add or take away something from the mix? Even if the skit is hilarious, there may be some changes you can make. Are there any ad-libs that need to become a permanent part of the skit? Are the actors out of control during a certain scene? With comedy, don't be afraid to "rein it in" a bit. A skit can go from hilarious to offensive in 0.8 seconds (0.01 seconds with a senior adult audience!).

3. **LET THE FAINT OF HEART STAY HOME WITH MOMMA.** Comedy is a tough gig. We believe it's more difficult to pull off than a drama, so take your comedy seriously! Comedy can also seem to go on forever because the actors want to milk the audience for every laugh they can get. In fact, good skits can easily go bad just because an actor thinks he's the best part of the program and takes over. And why not? Everyone is laughing! To avoid the never-ending-skit syndrome, time the skit beforehand and be aware of its length. One of the most difficult parts of producing a comedy is deciding when to say when—but you can't go wrong by leaving an audience wanting more.

"ADAM AND EVE"

BY EDDIE JAMES & TOMMY WOODARD WITH ANDREW DANIELS

WHAT: Was it easy for Adam and Eve to communicate? We have no way of knowing, but here's a fun look at how it might have gone when Adam tried to "hook up" with Eve. (Themes: Bible story, marriage, men and women, love)

WHO: Adam, Eve

WHEN: Shortly after, "In the beginning…"

WHY: Genesis 2:4-25; Proverbs 31:10; Ephesians 5:28-33

WEAR:
(COSTUMES AND PROPS)
Adam and Eve are wearing sandwich boards—both bearing the picture of a leaf—around their necks. Adam needs a piece of paper and pencil stashed on the underside of his front panel.

HOW: This skit portrays the difficulties of communication between men and women, and the more "modern" the actors play it, the better. The idea is to show ancient characters dealing with a contemporary issue, thus connecting the Bible with a modern audience.

---

*As the scene opens, **Adam** is onstage talking to himself and testing out his pick-up lines. **Eve** enters, but **Adam** doesn't see her until she says her first line.*

Adam: *(With "style")* Well, hello, Eve. Do you believe in love at first sight, or should I walk by one more time? Guess what? Cupid called and he wants to know why you stole my heart! Hey, is there an airport nearby, or is that the sound of my heart taking off? Are you from Tennessee? Because you're the only ten *I* see.

(Then, trying to talk himself out of being nervous) Come on, Adam, there's nothing to be afraid of, nothing to be nervous about. She's just a girl, just like every other girl in the world…

Eve: There are other girls in the world?

Adam: Eve! I, uh, didn't know you were around.

Eve: Just passing by. I didn't mean to scare you.

Adam: (*Bravado*) Scare me? You didn't scare me—I'm fearless. Besides, I knew you'd be coming this way.

Eve: You did?

Adam: Well, it's a small garden, and this is the only path in it. (*Eve looks unimpressed*) So…I used deductive reasoning and my private investigative skills to…

Eve: (*Interrupting Adam*) Okay, okay, I'm impressed.

Adam: You are?

Eve: Sure. I bet you can even tell me where I was going.

Adam: Absolutely. (*Looks around and nervously points in the opposite direction from where **Eve** is standing*) That way?

Eve: Good try. I'm going to the beach. Thought I'd try to name some more fish before it gets dark.

Adam: Sounds like fun. (*Awkward silence*) Guess I'll see you around.

Eve: Probably. See you later, Adam. (***Eve** begins to exit*)

Adam: (*Fumbling for words*) Eve, I was, uh, wondering…

Eve: (*Stops and turns around*) Wondering what?

Adam: If… (***Adam** turns toward the audience, smiling, his confidence and "style" returning*) I was wondering if your daddy was a thief because somebody must have stolen the stars and put them in your eyes.

Eve: Excuse me?

Adam: You know, if I could rearrange the alphabet, I'd put *U* and *I* together.

Eve: *What* are you talking about?

Adam: So did it hurt?

Eve: Did what hurt?

Adam: Did it hurt...when you fell from heaven?

Eve: Are you crazy? I didn't fall...

Adam: I did... (**Adam** *throws himself on the ground, landing on his stomach and leaning up, putting his hands under his chin*) I fell in love.

Eve: Adam, what's happened to you? Have you lost your mind, or are all men going to be this lousy at making conversation?

Adam: What do you mean?

Eve: Look, this has been a great talk, but I've got fish to name.

Adam: Think you could name one after me?

Eve: (*To self as she turns to leave*) Sure, it shouldn't be too hard to find a "dork-fish."

Adam: Eve, wait, I'm sorry. It's just...it's just that I get so nervous when I'm around you. I can't think straight. I don't know what to say. I mean, you're the most beautiful woman I've ever seen!

Eve: I'm the *only* woman you've ever seen.

Adam: You're right! I don't even look at other women!

Eve: Adam, I am the only woman on the entire planet!

Adam: Good point. But Eve, I need to ask you something, and it's probably the most important question I'll ever ask.

Eve: (*Looks at **Adam** strangely*) Okay...

Adam: (*Trying to build up confidence to say the words*) Will you…(*Pauses, can't get the words out*) Will you…(*After a couple tries, he reaches behind his "leaf" and pulls out the letter that's taped to the back of the panel*) Here, just read this.

Eve: (*Opens the letter and reads it aloud*) "Will you go out with me? Check yes or no." (*Looking at **Adam***) Adam…

Adam: I knew it. I'm not good enough for you. You know, I like poetry and knitting and walks on the beach…

Eve: Adam…

Adam: But you probably want a man who's bigger or stronger or taller or more athletic…

Eve: Adam…

Adam: You wouldn't even go out with me if I were the last man on earth.

Eve: (*Yelling*) Adam, you're the *first* man on earth (*a little calmer*) and the only man on earth. Now, if you'll let me finish…(***Adam*** *puts on a "pouty" face with his bottom lip out, sulking.* ***Eve*** *says next line with frustration*) Do you have a pencil? (***Adam*** *pulls out a pencil, and* ***Eve*** *looks at him strangely*) I bet that's uncomfortable.

Adam: Occasionally.

Eve: (*Makes a mark on the letter and hands it back to **Adam***) Here.

Adam: (*Covers his eyes and looks at the letter through open fingers. Is surprised at the response*) Yes. You said yes?

Eve: It's not like you have a lot of competition. (*To self*) It's not like you have *any* competition.

Adam: Wow, this is unbelievable! I can't believe it—I didn't think I had a chance. I sure hope future generations have an easier time figuring out women.

Eve: Future generations? Before we start talking about a family, let's make sure I survive the first date. So what are we going to do?

Adam: I could get some tickets…

Eve: Tickets to what?

Adam: (*Flexes muscles for* **Eve** *in numerous ways*) The *gun* show! (**Eve** *rolls her eyes and gives him the "what have I gotten myself into?" look*) Sorry.

Eve: Why don't we just start with something simple, like a picnic?

Adam: A picnic's good; I could do a picnic. (*Short pause*) What's a picnic?

Eve: It's where we bring food and sit in the grass and eat. Let's meet back here at six o'clock.

Adam: Now hold up, little lady. You know, I'm a pretty important guy. I can't go just any old time; I may have things to do. You'll have to let me check my schedule…

Eve: We could always cancel.

Adam: Six is good. Do I need to bring anything?

Eve: Why don't you bring a dessert? I'll take care of everything else.

Adam: Okay. Do you have any favorites?

Eve: How about an apple pie.

Adam: What's an apple?

Eve: Never mind, I'll bring that too. Just try to be here on time.

Adam: All right, I guess I'll see you at six then.

Eve: I guess you will. (**Adam** *exits, almost skipping, as* **Eve** *watches*) Compared to living with a man, I bet childbirth will be a piece of cake.

Adam: (*From offstage*) What's cake? (*Fast fade on lights or exit,* **Eve** *looks at* **Adam** *like he's a "dorkfish," and* **Adam** *follows, saying things like, "Seriously, what's cake?"*)

THE END.

"RESIST THE DEVIL"
BY EDDIE JAMES & TOMMY WOODARD

WHAT: The last thing the Devil wants is for Chris to grow closer to God, and he'll try anything to keep Chris distracted. (Themes: sin, temptation, victory in Christ)

WHO: Chris, Devil

WHEN: Present day

WHY: Luke 4:1-13; James 4:6-7; 1 Peter 5:8

WEAR: Index card, overcoat, two cell phones, pencil
(COSTUMES
AND PROPS)

HOW: The role of Chris could be played either by a man or a woman, though some dialogue will need to be altered to be gender-specific. The Devil should not be costumed in a way that suggests his identity.

Chris enters holding an index card.

Chris: I hate memorizing these Bible verses. They're always so hard for me. What's the point?

Devil: (*Surprises* **Chris**) All right, gimme your keys. This is a carjacking!

Chris: (*Scared*) A what?

Devil: This is a carjacking!

Chris: I'm not even in my car!

Pause. **Devil** *retools his tactics.*

Devil: Then take me to your car! I'm gonna steal your car!

Chris:	Okay.
Devil:	Where is it?
Chris:	(*Pointing*) About a mile that direction.
Devil:	(*Trying to eyeball it*) What kind of car is it?
Chris:	Pinto.
Devil:	Color?
Chris:	Avocado.
Devil:	Year?
Chris:	(*Name a year that's at least 20 years ago*)
Devil:	Forget it.

Chris, unsure of what just happened, goes back to memorizing. **Devil** pulls a pencil out of his pocket and holds it against **Chris's** back.

Devil:	All right, don't move an inch. I've got a knife to your back.
Chris:	A knife?
Devil:	Yeah. A big, sharp, *Braveheart*-type knife. One wrong move and I'll be performing major surgery on you.

Chris takes a slight step forward to get away from the knife.

Devil:	Hey! I told you not to move an inch! That was an inch. That was more than an inch.

Chris starts calling **Devil's** bluff, saying, "An inch? Like this? Like this?" Eventually, he turns around only to discover he was being held hostage by...

Chris:	A pencil? You were going to stab me with a pencil?
Devil:	Lead poisoning can be deadly.

Chris:	Is this some kind of joke?

Chris *goes back to his card.* ***Devil*** *puts a hand in his overcoat pocket and pretends to have a gun.*

Devil:	This is a stickup. Not joking this time. I have a gun. Now, give me your wallet.
Chris:	(*Starting to get wise*) How big is the gun?
Devil:	What?
Chris:	How big is the gun?
Devil:	(*Holds hands apart as if he were measuring a fish*) This big. (*He quickly puts his hand back in the coat pocket*) Now give me your wallet!

Chris *grabs the "gun" and twists the* ***Devil's*** *finger.* ***Devil*** *pulls away.*

Devil:	Owwww! (*Sucks finger*) I've got a bad hangnail. (*He assumes some kind of karate pose*) Don't mess with me. I know kay-ra-tay.
Chris:	You know what?
Devil:	Kay-ra-tay!
Chris:	(*Points over* ***Devil's*** *shoulder*) What's that? (***Devil*** *looks, and* ***Chris*** *knocks* ***Devil*** *to the ground. In the distance he sees someone*) Oh no, it's Ray.
Devil:	(*Sits up*) Who's Ray?
Chris:	Ray's this guy. All the girls want to be with him. All the guys want to be him. I mean everybody, everybody, *everybody* loves Raymond.
Devil:	Pretty cool guy, huh?
Chris:	Yeah.
Devil:	You couldn't hang with him. I mean, look at you.
Chris:	I know.

Devil: You're awkward. You certainly aren't as good looking. You can't even come close to being in his league.

Chris: I know, I…Wait a minute, that's not true. I'm a child of God. (**Devil** flinches) What? God? (**Devil** flinches again) I know who you are.

Devil: Yeah?

Chris: You're the devil.

Devil: Yeah…you got me. (Laughs) But you've gotta admit, I had you for a second there!

Chris: In fact, I was just reading about you.

Devil: Really? What did you read?

Chris: My memory verse. It says (reads card), "Resist the devil and he will flee."

Devil: What? Let me see that. Oh, that's an old verse. Things have changed since that was written.

Chris: No…I don't think so.

Devil: No?

Chris: No. You know what? I'm not going to listen to your lies and idle threats anymore. I am choosing to resist you. So go on, get out of here.

Devil: Yeah. I gotta go, but you're so easy. I had you so scared and worried and insecure…

Chris: Get outta here.

Devil: I'm going. But I'll be back. I'll be back.

Devil exits. **Chris's** cell phone rings.

Chris: (Into phone) Hello?

Devil: (Offstage as "Jimmie," disguising his voice) Hey, Chris.

Chris:	Jimmie! You'll never believe what just happened to me. I mean, I was walking to my car and…
Devil:	Yeah, yeah, yeah. I've got important news. Guess who just called me? Ray!
Chris:	Who?
Devil:	Ray.
Chris:	Ray? *Ray*-Ray?
Devil:	Yes.
Chris:	No way!
Devil:	Oh yeah. We're in!
Chris:	Are you serious?
Devil:	Why do you think I'm calling? Look, everyone's getting together at his house tonight, and we're there!
Chris:	That's great! (*Pause*) Wait a minute…I don't think we should go.
Devil:	Are you crazy? Everybody who's anybody will be there. We go, and we are *in* for the rest of our lives!
Chris:	Yeah, but won't there be…
Devil:	Chris, you're killing me here. Do you understand what's happening? This is what we've been waiting for. C'mon, you have to say yes to this.
Chris:	(*Mumbles*) Okay.
Devil:	What?
Chris:	(*Louder*) Okay. (*Starts to walk off, still talking on the phone*)

Devil enters while talking on a phone in *"Jimmie's"* voice.

Devil: This is gonna be so cool.

Chris: Yeah. Yeah. So what are you doing later...? (*Exits*)

Devil: (*Voice slowly changes back to normal*) A little this, a little that. (*Hangs up and looks at the audience*) Compromise—one of my favorite sins! Whenever you least expect me, expect me. I'll find you anytime, anywhere; and I'll use anyone to do it. It's only a matter of time. (*Chuckles to himself as he exits*)

THE END.

"HOLDING GRUDGES"

BY EDDIE JAMES & TOMMY WOODARD WITH BETH MCNELLEN

WHAT: Is forgiveness just a concept in your life, or is it a practice? This skit demonstrates how damaging grudges can be, and how withholding forgiveness can affect an entire family for generations. (Themes: family, forgiveness, bitterness, grudges)

WHO: Mom, Carrie, Dad

WHEN: Present day

WHY: Leviticus 19:18; Psalm 86:5; Matthew 6:14-15

WEAR:
(COSTUMES AND PROPS) Have family in "weekend clothes." Using a living room setting or a kitchen setting to draw the audience into the world you are trying to create can add a lot.

HOW: This skit can be a great way to add some adult actors into the mix with your students. Because it's just a simple conversation, it may lose some "believability" if students play the parent roles. The worst thing for this skit would be to play it up and exaggerate those roles.

---

*As the skit opens, **Mom, Dad,** and **Carrie** are sitting at a table together, making an invitation list for **Carrie's** upcoming graduation.*

Dad: All right, you have my full attention. Let's go over the list of people you want to invite to your graduation party.

Carrie: Okay, well, first of all, Grandma and Grandpa Miller, of course, and Grandpa Stuart...

Dad: Fine, fine.

Carrie: Dr. Kessler, Mrs. Kinder...

Dad: Uh huh.

Carrie:	The Collinses, the Bakers…
Dad:	Oh, oh, wait. Don't invite Dr. Kessler.
Carrie:	Dr. Kessler? But he delivered me, and…
Dad:	I know, I know, but after all the years we went to him, he turned me down flat when I finally got the courage to ask him to buy life insurance.
Mom:	I remember that. He turned you down flat!
Dad:	That's right.
Carrie:	Well, maybe he already had life insurance.
Dad:	And he couldn't afford more? The man drives a Porsche!
Mom:	Yeah, a Porsche!
Carrie:	Okay, okay. I just thought it would be cool if…(*Crosses off name*) No big deal. Mrs. Kinder. Mr. and Mrs. Collins. The Bakers. The Thomases…
Dad:	Mr. and Mrs. Collins?
Carrie:	Uh huh.
Mom:	Bill and Carol?
Carrie:	Yes.
Dad:	Uhh, we're not crazy about them.
Carrie:	You're not? They were my youth leaders!
Dad:	I know, I know. They're not *bad* people, but Carol made a reference to Mom's figure one time, and I didn't think that was…
Carrie:	Mom's figure?
Mom:	My legs.

Dad: She said your mom had skinny legs.

Mom: Chicken legs. She said I had chicken legs.

Dad: Sometimes she's tactless, that's all.

Carrie: (*Weakly*) He was a great youth leader.

Mom: He's only human.

Carrie: (*Sighs*) Okay. (*Crosses off another name*) The Bakers, the Thomases, Thelma Lukas and her sister, Louise. Mr. and Mrs....

Mom: Thelma Lukas?

Dad: You probably didn't know this, but Thelma Lukas suggested that we take you to a psychiatrist when you cut off all your hair in the fifth grade.

Carrie: But you *did* take me to a psychiatrist!

Mom: Not because *she* suggested it! What does she know about raising children?

Dad: She's never even been married!

Carrie: Well, should I invite her sister, then?

Dad: Honey, her sister had an affair with a married man. (*Sarcastically*) I suppose we should all just overlook that...

Carrie: She had an affair? She uses a walker!

Mom: It was years ago. Before you were born.

Carrie: And we're not inviting her to my graduation party because of it?

Dad: Honey, anytime you interact with people, you're going to have run-ins.

Carrie: Well then, scratch off Thelma and Louise. Now I've hardly got anyone left!

Mom:	That's not true.
Carrie:	Grandma and Grandpa Miller, Grandpa Stuart, Mrs. Kinder, and Uncle Marty. That's it—five people.
Dad:	Make that four people.
Carrie:	It's five, Dad.
Dad:	Uncle Marty can't come. And that's final.
Carrie:	But...Dad...he's your *brother*. He's my uncle.
Dad:	He also drinks like a fish, and he's not welcome here. End of discussion. We'll send him a picture.
Carrie:	Umm...okay.
Mom:	What about your best friend, Amy?
Carrie:	(*Matter of fact*) Amy didn't invite me to *her* graduation party.
Mom:	So?
Carrie:	So you think I'm going to invite her to mine?
Mom and Dad:	But honey, forgiveness is what our faith is all about!

*Lights fade as **Carrie** runs offstage, making frustrated growling noises.*

THE END.

"THE PSYCHIC?"

BY EDDIE JAMES & TOMMY WOODARD WITH ANDREW DANIELS

WHAT: Out on a blind date, a man tries a party trick that blows up in his face. Will he ever get a date again? (Themes: love, dating, communication, words)

WHO: Man, Woman

WHERE: Restaurant

WHEN: Present day

WHY: Proverbs 6:2-3; Ephesians 4:29; Hebrews 3:13

WEAR: Table, two chairs, plates, cups, tablecloth
(COSTUMES AND PROPS)

HOW: This is a fun skit about what happens when you volunteer to put your foot in your mouth. The best thing the actors can do is to play this as straight and normal as possible. Don't highlight the jokes; just say the lines, and the absurdity of the situation will connect with the audience.

---

*Man enters, looking around as if searching for someone. He sees **Woman** sitting at the table and walks over to her.*

Man: Excuse me—are you Cindy?

Woman: I am. And you must be Drew.

Man: That would be me. (*Sitting down*)

Woman: I'm sorry if I seem a little nervous; I've never been on a blind date before.

Man: I understand how you feel.

Woman:	Oh, is this your first blind date too?
Man:	No, but I haven't been on that many blind dates either. Maybe 25 or 30.
Woman:	Oh.
Man:	Well, it seems like things are going pretty smoothly so far.
Woman:	Yeah, at least we haven't had any of those awkward moments of silence.

Awkward moment of silence.

Man:	Except for that one.

Both laugh uncomfortably.

Woman:	So, I noticed you picked me out pretty easily.
Man:	It was easy; I simply looked for the most beautiful woman in the restaurant.
Woman:	That is so sweet!
Man:	And then I noticed someone was already sitting with her.
Woman:	Oh.
Man:	And then I saw you sitting here. You looked so lonely, like somebody who would go out on a blind date. So I figured this would be a good place to start.
Woman:	(*Under breath*) Well, having been on 30 blind dates, I guess you'd be the *expert* at knowing what to look for.
Man:	Well, it worked, didn't it?
Woman:	Yeah, I guess it did. So, what do you do for a living?
Man:	I'm a psychic.
Woman:	Really?

Man:	Actually I'm a psychic in training, but I'll be finished soon.
Woman:	How fascinating! I didn't realize they had training programs for psychics. But then again, I've never been to a real psychic; I've only seen those flunkies who work the carnival circuits. What school did you go to?
Man:	Mostly I just work the carnival circuit.
Woman:	Oh…
Man:	And fairs…sometimes…I…work the fairs.
Woman:	Well, there's nothing like on-the-job training!

*Another awkward moment of silence ensues, with both **Man** and **Woman** trying to avoid eye contact.*

Man:	That's what my mom always said. Anyway, they say everyone's got a little psychic in them. Why don't we see if it's true?
Woman:	What?
Man:	Try to guess my age.
Woman:	I couldn't.
Man:	Come on, it'll be fun.
Woman:	No, I don't want to.
Man:	Come on…just give it a shot…what's it going to hurt?
Woman:	Okay. I'd say you're…28.
Man:	Wow! You're right on the money. See, that wasn't so bad. Maybe you should be the psychic.
Woman:	I don't know about that.
Man:	No, I'm serious. I get the sense that you may really have the gift!

Woman:	Really? How cool! (*Relaxing, beginning to enjoy the date for the first time*) Okay, now let's put your skills to the test. How old do you think I am?
Man:	I'm not sure I'm ready for this. I'm still in training, and I'm not that good yet.
Woman:	(*Flirtatiously*) How hard can it be?
Man:	I really need more practice.
Woman:	(*Flirting more and more*) Come on…just guess! Like you said, what can it hurt?
Man:	Okay. Give me a minute here. (*Shakes out his hands, takes in three deep breaths, rolls his eyes back in his head*) I'll say you're…37.
Woman:	(*Shocked*) What?
Man:	I told you I'm still in training.
Woman:	You can't be serious. You can't really think I'm 37?
Man:	You're right. Let me take another shot. You're 39.
Woman:	I am not 39. I am nowhere near 39.
Man:	49?
Woman:	(*Angry*) You're moving in the wrong direction.
Man:	Okay…36?
Woman:	No.
Man:	35…34…33?
Woman:	I'm one year younger than you. I'm 27.
Man:	I told you I wasn't very good.
Woman:	You certainly weren't lying.

Man:	But you know what I am good at...
Woman:	(*Wanting to leave*) I'm sure I'd never guess.
Man:	Guessing people's weight. That's where I got my start.
Woman:	Why am I not surprised?
Man:	Would you mind standing up for a second, just so I can get a good look?
Woman:	Whatever.

Woman *stands and turns.*

Man:	All right. I'd say you weigh in at a good 185.
Woman:	Excuse me?
Man:	Was I off by much?

Woman *is stunned.*

Woman:	Were you off by much?
Man:	How about 195...?

Woman *stands to leave.*

Man:	The big 2-1-0...?

Woman *starts to walk away.*

Man:	Come on, I bet your scale reads at least 200...

Woman *stops and returns to table.*

Woman:	How about I give you one more chance to redeem yourself?
Man:	I'm game.

Woman: (*Sarcastically*) Why don't you use your psychic powers to see if we'll have a second date? But this time close your eyes—your powers might work better that way.

Man: Good idea.

Man closes eyes. *Woman* stands up, slaps *Man* across the face, and storms out.

Man: (*Rubbing face*) Wow, I didn't see that coming!

THE END.

"THE WAY WE PRAY"

BY EDDIE JAMES & TOMMY WOODARD

WHAT: As this skit demonstrates, the real key to prayer is being genuine. What God really desires is a two-way conversation with us. (Themes: prayer, listening to God, worship)

WHO: God, Characters 1 through 6

WHEN: Present day

WHY: Matthew 6:9-13, 25-34; Luke 11:5-13; John 17:11-19

WEAR: This skit looks best when each character is costumed and carrying appropriate
(COSTUMES   props (listed in each scene). Small creative touches will go a long way.
AND PROPS)

HOW: This skit consists of a large cast, but with creative casting (having actors play more than one character), it can be adapted to a duet. Also, a key element to this skit is the change of accents or voices from character to character.

Character 1 begins to pray, speaking in a normal voice.

Character 1:   God?

God: I'm right here.

Character 1:   Hi, it's me, and, uh, I know we haven't talked in a long time, but I've been trying really hard to get down just the right words and everything, but now I think I've finally got them down, and you're really going to be pleased with them, and so, uh, here I go, with my prayer.

(*Switches to snooty, King James, "preacher" voice with British accent*) Oh, Heavenly Father, Oh, Heavenly Father, I beseech Thee not unto Thee, oh, Heavenly Father…(*Trying to think of new things to say*) How now, brown cow? (*Becomes more wound up and intent*) Oh, my soul is dry and parched, but if I could just catch a morsel of who You are…(*thinking*) so verily, merrily…down the stream! Oh, love me, love me, say that you love me…

God: Just talk to me…

Character 1: (*Interrupts*) Oh, Heavenly Father!

God: Just talk to me normally.

Character 1: (*Interrupts*) Oh, yes! Thine has heard mine prayer! I'm a poet and did not know it. Ahmen.

God: There's so much more I wanted to tell you.

For **Character 2,** *use a lazy, slacker, "skater"-type teenager voice. Needs folded piece of paper in his pocket or on his lap.*

Character 2: Uh, God?

God: I'm here.

Character 2: Hey. Um, look, I know I haven't talked to you in a while and everything, but I got kind of, some problems. Like, uh, I got a quiz tomorrow, and tonight (*use title of popular TV show that this character would watch*) is on, and it's a conflict, if you know what I mean. So if you could just, like, give me total recall of everything I've learned in class, that'd be really cool. Especially those days I skipped. Um, also, uh, there's that girl who I like, uh, *Stacy*, heh. (*Throat, lion growl*) You did really good with her! Created in your image all right. She's a goddess. Yeah, um, if you could make it so that when she looks at me she sees someone really handsome instead of, uh, me—that would be really cool, too. All right? And, uh, hold on—I wrote down some things. (*Unfolds piece of paper and reads list*) Hmmm, oh yeah, uh, my car—it's a Chevette (*or some other bad car*). Could you, uh, make it, like, *not* a Chevette? Pretty much anything else would do. Um, also, my mom…I want to lift her up to you and ask you to…get her off my back? Could you make her, like, mute for a day? You know, don't hurt her, or anything permanent (*pause*), for now. (*Looks back at list, then laughs*) What am I thinking—you can read! (*Holds the list up, as if showing it to God. Pauses for a moment, and then laughs again*) Oh, I guess you're probably a speed-reader. (*Brings list back down*) Okay, uh, thanks, bye!

God: There was so much more I wanted to tell you!

Character 3 is a weepy, whiny person, wringing hands and complaining.

Character 3: God?

God: Yes, I'm here.

Character 3: Hi, it's me, and um… (*bursts into tears*) I'm sorry. I'm crying, I didn't want to cry and now I'm crying…(*sniffs loudly*) I just can't stop crying! I feel like my life is in the toilet and Satan has his hand on the flusher (*makes flushing sound*)…you know what I'm saying? I mean, I didn't think it was gonna be this way when I gave everything over to you! I mean, why? Why does stuff have to happen? You know, like, I'm walking through the park the other day, minding my own business, and this dog just comes right up and grabs my leg, all (*makes growling sound*). Why? Why? I didn't need that, you know? And then, I go to take my driver's test, but I didn't have a number two pencil, so I asked the instructor for one, and he throws it at me, and it sticks me right in the eye, and I'm bleeding and—why? You know? I didn't need that! I didn't need that at all. So I can't drive, and I have to catch the school bus; but instead, the bus *hits* me—why? What's that about? I just don't get it! And, um, and, um (*calms down*), my dad, um, he slept on the couch again last night. My mom and dad, they just keep fighting and fighting, and I don't know what's going on. If they get a divorce…I mean, do you even care what's going on with me?

God: Oh yeah. I care more than you do.

Character 3: Then why is it that every time I pray, I feel like my prayers are just bouncing off the ceiling?

God: They're not; that's just the way you feel. I hear everything you're saying.

Character 3: What's the use?

God: No…

Character 3: (*Interrupts*) What's the use? Amen.

God: There was so much more I wanted to tell you.

Character 4 is an example of those who make prayer a big production for other people to see. When the "prayer" begins, Character 4 sings every word in the style of a current worship song.

Character 4:   God?

God: I'm here!

Character 4:   (*Giggles, then closes eyes and begins to sing, making it up on-the-fly and acting out the song with hand and arm movements*) God, I'm here (*pause*), God, draw near! (*Giggles, proud of the rhyme*) Come to me, my Father, 'cause I looove yooou! You are so grandiose, and I am so "tinymose"! You are the One for all tiiiime! You're my Master, my Savior, I looove yooou! Mighty God! Mighty God! (*Pause—huge arm movements*) Mighty GOD!

(*Stops singing and assumes a Pharisee pose*) Look at me, world! I'm praying!

God: Yes, but to whom?

Character 4:   (*Closes eyes and sings again*) Ahh-haahh-haaah-MENNNN! (*Takes elaborate bow*)

God: There was so much more I wanted to tell you.

Character 5 is a sleepy person trying to pray before drifting off.

Character 5:   (*Mumbling*) Uh, God?

God: Yes, I'm right here.

Character 5:   (*Yawning*) Hi, um, it's me, and um (*stretches*), I thought I'd talk to you before I go to bed tonight, and uh, I just want to tell you that, uh…(*Drifts off to sleep, snorts awake*) I love you, I love you very much, and uh…(*Drifts off again, head falls forward*)

(*Wakes up, shaking head to clear it, and tries again*) And God, thanks for all you've done for me, and I really want to be salt, and I really want to be light, and (*eyes closing again*) I just want to be light and salt and salt and light and pepper and oregano…(*Begins to snore, wakes up, wipes drool off face*) Uh, yeah, God, just really help me to be all I can be for you, 'cause that's what I wanna do and be and…(*Drops head back, begins to snore again*)

God:	Hey, are you there?
Character 5:	Oh yeah, God, I'm sorry, I was saying…*(Falls completely asleep)*
God:	There was so much more I wanted to tell you.

Character 6 is sincerely praying, and this scene should not be played for laughs.

Character 6:	God?
God:	I'm here.
Character 6:	I love you. You're greater than anything I could ever hope for.
God:	I love you, too.
Character 6:	Listen, I can't wait for you to come back and get us. I mean, I really can't. But until that time comes, would you help me to live my life as if I were already in heaven, with you?
God:	I will. But you need to trust me, on a daily basis—not just when you're in a crisis or your life is falling apart—but daily. I desire that. I look at your heart, nothing else.
Character 6:	I've got a lot of needs down here. I just need your help. I need to know that you're going to meet those needs and help me.
God:	I know every one of your needs. I know them better than you do, and I know them before you ask. It saddens me at times when you take the reins away from me and try to do things on your own. Will you trust me—not just 25 percent of your trust, but 100 percent—even when things don't seem like they're going your way? I'm in control, and I know your needs; let me provide.
Character 6:	Yes. Oh, uh, speaking of needs, I need you to forgive me. I've already blown it so many times today. Please forgive me.
God:	I forgive you, and I've forgotten it. You're the only one beating yourself up. Put the club down. I want to do things with your life, but I can't because you continually beat yourself up for your past. Just stop. Let it go and give it to me…now.

Character 6:	But this world is just filled with spiritual potholes. I'll be walking the right way, and then suddenly, *boom*, I blow it. Help me to just…
God:	Shhhhh…
Character 6:	…Help me to just…
God:	Shhhh.
Character 6:	Excuse me?
God:	You talk way too much. Most of my children do. They never take time to listen to me. Always so busy. There is nothing that you and I can't handle together. You do the possible; allow me to do the impossible with your life. I want to. Trust me.
Character 6:	Hey, it's just us. I'd like to praise you, if that's okay.
God:	I'd love that.
Character 6:	(*Begins to sing "I Could Sing of Your Love Forever" or another current worship song*)
God:	You're finally getting the hang of this.
Character 6:	(*Keeps singing until song is finished*)

THE END

DRAMA  3.0

A RUN FOR THE OSCARS

Why all the drama? Can someone please tell me why there is so much drama in this chapter? Oh my, why is everyone so dramatic?

It's a fact: If you're working with "theater people," no doubt you've got quite enough drama in your life. It truly does come with the territory, but it isn't their fault; that's the way God made them. The key, however, is to channel that drama from real life—where it drives people nuts—to the stage, where it can actually be inspiring.

That's the goal of the skits in this chapter. Each one is full of meat and, well, drama. Some will make you cry; some will make you ache; some may even make you feel uncomfortable—but they'll all make you think. With these skits, you'll want to use your best actors—your "go-to" people or the ones you know can play it *up* without *over*playing it.

Keep in mind that some of these skits don't ride off into the sunset. They're designed to feel more like real life where people don't always choose to do the right thing in the end. Also, as in real life, these skits may contain some humor. Like the drama, the humor should be played more naturally, not over-the-top.

Be careful with your dramatic skits. They'll either be the best thing you do or the worst; with drama, there's often no middle ground.

SKIT TIPS

1. **DON'T ACT LIKE A RECENTLY GROUNDED 13-YEAR-OLD GIRL.** Actors in a dramatic role often end up overacting by exaggerating their expressions and movements. They yell when a whisper would be more powerful. They say and do things no sane person would say or do in real life. We're not pointing fingers here; it's natural to want

to make a dramatic role a heavier performance. The key is to remember the golden rule in drama: *Less is more.* Let the script provide the drama—to overdo it is to kill it.

2. **NOT "WWJD?" BUT "WWTCD?"** In life, it's always a good idea to put ourselves aside and try to behave as Jesus would. But on the stage, we need to choose to inhabit *the character* we're playing, put our own opinions and reactions away, and even give Jesus a rest. (Unless you're playing the role of Jesus—in which case, WWJD? your little heart out!) The question is not how would *you* react to a situation or say the dialogue, but how would *that character* do or say it? This is a difficult distinction to make, but one that's critical to drama. We tend to put ourselves in the *situation* instead of putting ourselves in the *character*. If someone walks away from your performance and thinks they've just watched *you* get mad and yell onstage, then you've missed the mark. But if audience members can lose themselves in the person you're playing, then you've accomplished your goal.

3. **HURRY UP AND SLOW DOWN!** We know that doesn't make sense, but it got your attention, right? The point is to slow down. Too often actors tend to rush through the skit, zipping dialogue back and forth until the scene sounds more like Ping-Pong™ with words. Try to take the scene at the appropriate rhythm and tempo of a real-life scenario. In most cases, that means to go slower than you think you should. By the way, while you're slowing down, don't be afraid to shut your trap and let your face do some acting. Don't tell us what happened; show us with your eyes and facial expressions.

4. **ROBERT DE NIRO AND MERYL STREEP YOU ARE NOT.** What is it about stepping onto a stage that turns a lot of actors into Shakespearean rejects with British accents? A major *faux pas* of dramatic acting is the distortion of dialogue due to over-enunciation. With dramas, the more naturally you speak, the better it will come across. Most of us haven't been to Juilliard and we aren't flipping through this book between Broadway casting calls, so just be natural. Think about how your character would speak, and try not to chew up your dialogue until it's unrecognizable. The more relaxed you are, the more realistic your character will be.

"DIRTY ROSE"

BY EDDIE JAMES & TOMMY WOODARD WITH THE SKITIOTS

WHAT: When Aaron discovers the truth about Mandy's past, he wants out of their relationship, but God desires a pure and restored relationship with Mandy. (Themes: dating, forgiveness, past, God's love)

WHO: Aaron, Mandy, God

WHEN: Present day

WHY: Luke 6:37; Ephesians 1:7-8

WEAR: Two white roses
(COSTUMES AND PROPS)

HOW: Really get your actors to see where each character is coming from. This is a good opportunity to highlight how God's forgiveness through Christ is once and for all, and even though people put conditions on their love for others, God's love is unconditional.

Aaron enters with a white rose behind his back. Mandy is waiting for him.

Aaron: Hey, we need to talk.

Mandy: Okay. What about?

Aaron shows her the rose, and she looks happily at it, reaching for it.

Aaron: Actually I wasn't going to give this to you. I wanted to use it to show you something.

Mandy: Show me what? What's going on?

Aaron: Listen…I don't think this is going to work out.

Mandy: (*Disappointed and confused*) Um…okay…

Aaron: Here's the thing. I found out about everything you did last year before we got together, and I don't know if I can be with someone who has that kind of past.

Mandy: But, I'm not like that anymore. I don't understand why that changes anything now.

Aaron: (*Sincerely*) See this rose? This represents your purity. It's newly cut and (*smells it*) still smells fresh. But if I were to take this rose and let a lot of people touch it, smell it, hold it—it wouldn't look the same. (*Crumples the rose*) It would probably look something more like this. God didn't give us this perfect white rose for us to just give it away. Now look at it.

Mandy: (*To herself*) That's not true.

Aaron: Not true? I think it is. Be honest, Mandy. Are you or are you not guilty of your past? Are the things everyone's saying true or not?

Mandy: (*Nods*) Yes.

Aaron: Okay, then. Look at this rose. Now it's dirty and broken. Mandy, who's going to want a dirty rose? (*Exits*)

Mandy: (*Stunned, begins to pray*) God, I'm so sorry. He's right. I *am* guilty. I *did* do those things. He has every right to be mad at me, and so do you. I don't deserve your forgiveness for the things I've done. He's right…I'm just a dirty rose, and who's going to want a dirty rose?

God enters with a new white rose behind his back.

God: I do!

Mandy: God, I am so sorry…

God: (*Interrupts*) Mandy, I don't condemn you. It's okay. I want you and accept you just as you are.

Mandy: But God, you don't understand everything that happened.

God: Mandy, my love for you covers all those things. You're what I came for. That's how deep my love is. It heals and restores you from the inside out (*hands her the new rose*) and makes you brand new. (*They embrace*) Now go in peace. Not regret, but peace.

(***Mandy*** *exits.* ***God*** *picks up the dirty rose and addresses the audience*)

Who wants this dirty rose? I do! This is why I sent my Son to die for everyone—because everyone is a dirty rose at some point in his life. That's what sin does: It ruins and destroys everything it touches, and it makes everyone broken, bent, unlovable, and nasty at the core. But this is my good news: I love you as you are right now. Every single person in this room is a dirty rose that's stained and damaged, but I sent my Son to put you back together and breathe new life into you. Just as I told Mandy, "Go in peace," I want you to leave this room in peace—not in regret or in shame. Go in peace knowing that I alone can forgive and restore. Go in peace knowing that I can heal your heart. But more importantly, go in peace knowing that I love you right now, just as you are! Who wants this dirty rose? (*Pause*) I do!

THE END.

SKIT 3.2

"SORRY SEEMS TO BE THE HARDEST WORD"
BY EDDIE JAMES & TOMMY WOODARD WITH BRIAN CROPP

WHAT: As friends Kim and Jenny grow up, Jenny struggles to understand and cope with her parents' divorce. Will she ever be able to forgive and find some healing? (Themes: parents, forgiveness, hurt, healing)

WHO: Kim, Jenny

WHEN: Present day

WHY: Genesis 50:17; Matthew 6:15; Colossians 3:13

WEAR: Dolls, schoolbooks
(COSTUMES AND PROPS)

HOW: This sketch involves scene changes that happen pretty quickly. One way to illustrate these changes is by differing the lighting. Also, use small physical changes to portray how the actors are growing older, such as pigtails for childhood, ponytails for the teenage years, and loose hair for the college scene. Actors may also portray these transitions with language and behavior characterizations.

Jenny and *Kim* are playing with their dolls. It's teatime.

Jenny: (*In doll voice*) Come on in, Betty Sue. Sit down and have some tea.

Kim: I don't wanna play anymore. Y'wanna go outside and play with your dog?

Jenny: No, 'cause that icky, creepy kid is next door.

Kim: So...

Jenny: So he's always out playing in the mud, or eating the dog food, or blowing up his toys.

Kim:	So we'll just ignore him.
Jenny:	You can't ignore him. He's got like this thing around him, like, uh, like a germ bubble!
Kim:	Yeah?
Jenny:	Uh huh, and if he gets near you, your skin starts to peel off your face, and you lie there faceless and helpless (*makes agonizing sounds and writhes on the floor*), until you die a painful death (*pretends to die*).
Kim:	Couldn't you just call for help?
Jenny:	You have no mouth. Your face just fell off, remember?
Kim:	So you don't wanna go outside?
Jenny:	No.
Kim:	Okay.

Jenny silently plays with her dolls for a moment, while *Kim* sits and plays with the hem of her shirt.

Kim:	You ever think you'll get married?
Jenny:	Mom says it's (*mispronounce*) inevitable.
Kim:	What's that mean?
Jenny:	I don't know, but it can't be good. Imagine being stuck with that new kid forever.
Both:	YECHK!
Jenny:	Who do you want to marry?
Kim:	I dunno…(*Current hot male celebrity*) is cute.
Jenny:	Josh is cute.

Kim:	Josh is gross. The other day, the other day at lunch, I was standing in line talking to Shannon, and he tapped me on the shoulder. So I turned…and he farted right on us.
Jenny:	Gross.
Kim:	Of course he and his friends thought it was funny.
Jenny:	That's why I'm not getting married.
Kim:	You're not?
Jenny:	My dad told me there isn't a boy alive who will be good enough for me.
Kim:	You believe him?
Jenny:	Why shouldn't I?
Kim:	Because there's like a gobble-gillion people in this world, there's gotta be *somebody* you can marry.
Jenny:	Uh huh. Even if there was, my guy is probably living in China and we'll never meet. Besides, Dad was really messed up after Mom left. That's not gonna happen to me.

Scene Two: *The girls are now teenagers, taking a quiz out of a teen magazine.*

Jenny:	What did you score?
Kim:	Um…43.
Jenny:	You are…you are…(*Reads, laughs*) It says you are "deeply devoted." (*Reading*) "The deeply devoted woman is passionately loyal to her interests. While this should be admired, watch out! Deeply devoted women are often unable to be objective in relationships."
Kim:	Who wants to be obje…
Jenny:	Objective.
Kim:	What's that again?

Jenny: Able to see both sides.

Kim: I can see both sides. (*Pause*) What did you score?

Jenny: "Fraidy cat."

Kim: What's that?

Jenny: Says I'm scared of getting too close to people too quickly.

Kim: Are you sure?

Jenny: That's what it says. But who can believe a stupid teen magazine? (*Pause*)

Kim: So what are you doin' after graduation?

Jenny: My mom wants to spend some "quality time" with me before I go to college.

Kim: Wow, for how long?

Jenny: Too long. I mean, it's stupid—she left when I was seven and barely kept in touch. Now all of a sudden when I'm almost on my own, she wants to come back and play mother to me.

Kim: Maybe she's changed.

Jenny: *My* mother? Please. No, I'll probably go over there, then she'll try to "make up for lost time," and she'll just mess with my brain—which will be a really good first step going in to college.

Kim: You should give her a chance.

Jenny: Why?

Kim: She's your mother.

Jenny: Maybe, but she won't ever be my mom. (*long pause*)

Kim: Have you thought any more about what we talked about?

Jenny:	About…?
Kim:	About God?
Jenny:	(*Sighs*) I wish you'd lay off. I'm sorry; I know it's important to you, but I just can't right now.
Kim:	I'm just thinkin' you need to forgive your mom.
Jenny:	Well, maybe, but I can't.
Kim:	You can't because you need forgiveness; you need to be loved.
Jenny:	What do you know about it? You've lived with both of your parents.
Kim:	C'mon, we've been friends since forever; I know what it's like. And I know you need to let go and forgive her.
Jenny:	I can't, okay?
Kim:	It's not gonna get any better 'til you do. (*long pause*)
Jenny:	So if I believe, I'll be able to forgive my mother?
Kim:	If you believe in Jesus…
Jenny:	(*Cuts her off*) Maybe later.

Scene Three: *Several years have passed, and the girls are now in college. Jenny enters.*

Kim:	Hey.
Jenny:	You're still up?
Kim:	Are you kidding me? Dr. Mitchell's Western Civilization paper is due Monday. Of course I'm up.

Jenny sits down, obviously disturbed about something.

Kim:	You wanna talk about it?

Jenny:	What's to talk about? She picked me up; we had dinner; she dropped me off.
Kim:	That's it? You didn't talk?
Jenny:	Oh, we talked. Or should I say, she talked. (*Mocking her mom's voice*) "So, gosh, wow, you're in college? Wow, what's your major? Wow, wow, wow."
Kim:	Wow.
Jenny:	Tell me about it. It's like she doesn't even know me, like I was never her daughter or something. Stupid.
Kim:	What can I do for you?
Jenny:	Nothin.' I'll be fine.
Kim:	No, you won't. You haven't been fine since she left. (*Jenny gives Kim a look*) I'm serious. Forgive her.
Jenny:	What?
Kim:	You heard me. Forgive her.
Jenny:	You don't know what you're talking about.
Kim:	You've been a jerk to me sometimes, and I've forgiven you.
Jenny:	Yeah, but you're better than me.
Kim:	Look, we're like sisters. You know me. You know my strengths and weaknesses. You've been with me through my ups and downs. You know I'm not better than you. The only difference between you and me…
Jenny:	I know, I know.
Kim:	He'll take away that hurt. He'll be the comfort you need. He'll be whatever you need him to be.
Jenny:	If that's the case, then why hasn't he seen to it that my mom's…

Kim: I said he'll be what you need him to be, not what you *think* you need. I don't know why your mom's like she is. But you're my best friend, and I want you to have the peace and joy that I have.

Jenny: (*Pause*) I'm so afraid.

Kim: Of what?

Jenny: I'm afraid I'm going to turn out like my mom. That's why I've never let my guard down with anyone. Guess that test we did back in high school was right. I really am a "fraidy cat." Maybe it'll be impossible for me to experience love the way it should be. Just impossible.

Kim: I know...

Jenny: Impossible!

Kim: I know...

Jenny: Did you hear me? I said there's no way. I said it's impossible.

Kim goes back to her homework. Jenny paces a little, sits, and stares at Kim. Finally...

Kim: I know...(*Jenny gives Kim another look*) I know a God who deals in impossibilities...It's just up to you to do the possible. Give the hurt over to God, Jenny. (*As they start to talk, the lights fade*)

THE END.

"THE BIRDCAGE"

BY EDDIE JAMES & TOMMY WOODARD

SKIT 3.3

WHAT: A metaphor for the trap of sin, "The Birdcage" reveals how easy it is to become trapped, and how Jesus gave his life to set us free. (Themes: salvation, grace, freedom in Christ)

WHO: Boy/Satan, Man/Jesus

WHEN: Any time

WHY: Luke 4:18-21; Romans 8:31-39; Revelation 20:10

WEAR: A birdcage with a cloth to cover it. Boy should wear a baseball cap to the side to appear youthful.
(COSTUMES AND PROPS)

HOW: This skit is very funny, but with a clever spin as it takes a serious turn. Play it for laughs during the first scene, but then strive for sincerity during the second scene to allow the audience to feel the weight of the message.

---

*As the scene opens, **Boy** enters carrying a birdcage covered by a cloth. As he walks he bumps into **Man**. **Man** has been looking for something.*

Man: Excuse me, what's that you've got there?

Boy: Just some wild birds I caught.

Man: Really. Where'd you catch them?

Boy: Over in that field.

Man: Well, what are you going to do with those wild birds?

Boy: I'm gonna play games with them.

Man:	Games? What kind of games do you play with wild birds?
Boy:	I poke a stick at 'em, and I scare 'em, and I make 'em fight with each other. Sometimes I shake their cage. That's what I do.
Man:	What are you gonna do with them when you're done playing with them?
Boy:	I'm gonna feed 'em to my cat. I got a cat that loves wild birds.
Man:	Actually, I had some birds fly away from me. I think those are my birds.
Boy:	Finders keepers, losers weepers.
Man:	Those are my birds.
Boy:	Describe them.
Man:	Beautiful birds with bright feathers and a beautiful song.
Boy:	That's them. Five dollars.
Man:	What?
Boy:	Ten dollars.
Man:	You're making me buy back my own birds?
Boy:	Twenty dollars, and that's my final offer.
Man:	Twenty dollars?
Boy:	Yeah…they're exotic birds.
Man:	You found them in a field.
Boy:	So? It was an exotic field.
Man:	Right. Okay, here's your twenty dollars. That's quite a sacrifice, you know.

Boy:	Whatever. (*Boy takes the money and gives the cage to the* **Man***. Then he walks away*)
Man:	(*Opens cage*) There you go. Go on now, you're free. (*Sings*) Jesus loves me this I know, for the Bible tells me so. Little ones to him belong; they are weak, but he is strong…(*Covers up the cage and sets it on the ground*)

At this point the mood shifts to a spiritual scene. **Man** *becomes* **Jesus***, and* **Boy** *becomes* **Satan***. (Use vocal and physical qualities to differentiate these characters from the* **Man** *and* **Boy***.)* **Satan** *enters.*

Satan:	I see you're looking at the cage.
Jesus:	Yeah, what's in there?
Satan:	Humans.
Jesus:	Humans? Where did you find them?
Satan:	In the Garden. (*Pause*) The funny thing is, I didn't put them in the cage; they put themselves in there.
Jesus:	What are you going to do with them now that they're in the cage?
Satan:	Going to play games with them.
Jesus:	What kind of games?
Satan:	Games they think will bring them lots of pleasure, but will really leave them totally empty. I'm going to make right seem wrong, and wrong seem right.
Jesus:	What next?
Satan:	They'll be damned for all eternity. What else would happen to them?
Jesus:	How about freedom?
Satan:	Oh yeah…freedom. Do you know what these humans will do if you give them freedom?

Jesus:	Yes.
Satan:	You know they're no good. They've turned their backs on you before, and they'll do it again.
Jesus:	At least they'll have a choice.
Satan:	You're serious?
Jesus:	Very serious.
Satan:	How far are you willing to go? Tears?
Jesus:	Yes.
Satan:	Your blood?
Jesus:	Yes.
Satan:	Your life? That's quite a sacrifice. Are you willing to give your life?
Jesus:	Yes. (*Opens the cage*) There you go. You're free. Free to live the way my Father intended. Free. Free.

Jesus watches humanity fly in freedom, smiles, and exits.

*Optional closing: After **Jesus** has opened the cage and shown that it is now empty, the actor looks at the audience and says…*

Actor:	Maybe this describes you right now. You feel like you're in a prison, and you want to be set free. Christ came to give us freedom. He wants you to be free to live life as he intended. Don't miss the opportunity to find out about the freedom he bought for you with his life.

THE END.

"LOST AND FOUND"
THE STORY OF THE PRODIGAL SON
BY EDDIE JAMES & TOMMY WOODARD

SKIT
3.4

WHAT: Through the eyes of both father and son, one of Jesus' most powerful parables comes to life. (Themes: forgiveness, rebellion, redemption, parental love)

WHO: Father, Son

WHEN: Present day

WHY: Luke 15:11-32; Romans 4:7; 1 John 3:1

WEAR: None
(COSTUMES AND PROPS)

HOW: This skit is actually more like two monologues woven together. It's best presented with both actors facing the audience and rarely looking at each other. The stage should be completely black with the only lighting being spots on the actors.

Son: Do you ever get bored with your average, day-to-day existence? I sure do. Well, I should say, I *did*. Then I decided to do something about it. You see, conventional wisdom says that you live your life, and then when you're older, your parents pass away, and you get whatever they have left—an inheritance. I'm sorry, but that just isn't good enough. I mean, come on. Give me the money now so I can really enjoy it! So here's what I did—I walked right up to my dad, and I said…

Father: "Dad, I want what's coming to me right now." That's what my younger son said to me. "What's coming to me"? Right at that moment, I was thinking, *Yeah, I'll give you what's coming to you!* Who does he think he is, demanding things from me? I brought him into this world, and I can take him out and make another one just like him! (*Softening*) But, he's my son, and I love him. And as much as it pained me, I decided to give him what he asked for and let him search for a better life on his own. Not long after that, he packed his bags, and the next thing I knew…

Son:	I was outta there! Kissed that boring place goodbye! There was a whole world out there waiting for me to discover it. So the first thing I did was…
Father:	He got lost. Hey, I love him, but he's no Magellan. In fact, I heard he had to stop four times for directions before he got out of our hometown.
Son:	That's not true! (**Father** looks in **Son's** direction) It was three times. And one of those doesn't count because I couldn't understand what that one guy was saying; I just nodded my head and left. And besides that, the only reason I wasn't good with directions is because *someone* never took the time to teach me…(**Son** motions with his head toward **Father**)
Father:	Don't go there.
Son:	Anyway, that doesn't really matter. The point is, I did find my way out of town—and then I began to live it up! I had it all! I had more friends than I knew what to do with and the best clothes money could buy, I was eating like a king, and the ladies…What can I say about the ladies?
Father:	Here's what I can say: None of them were ladies. Oh, they may have been women, but they weren't ladies.
Son:	They were too ladies! Well…most of them. Okay, there was Sheila…and Nancy…yeah, they weren't really ladies…and Becca…and Margo…hmm, come to think of it—none of them were ladies.
Father:	As I was saying…
Son:	Wait! Connie! Now Connie was a lady!
Father:	Yeah, a lady of the evening.
Son:	Okay, never mind…none of them were ladies. But the friends, the clothes, the food! Man, they were awesome! (*Pause*) Until…
Father:	His money ran out right about the time the whole country hit a recession.
Son:	There wasn't any work to be found. Man, I tried…I really did, but I couldn't find work. I searched and searched, and finally I got a job as a manager… (**Father** makes a buzzer noise to indicate his son is lying) Well,

not really a manager, but an associate... (**Father** *makes buzzer sound again*) Okay, okay, I was a bacon preparation assistant.

Father: Which means...

Son: I took care of pigs. (*Pause*) I couldn't believe my life had come to this. I'd wasted everything my father had given me. I wasn't really making any money to speak of; I had no place to live; I had no food to eat. There were days when I would've eaten the disgusting scraps I had to feed the pigs...but I couldn't. They wouldn't let me. So with hunger pains as a constant reminder of how I'd squandered my life away, I lived a life of misery...day after day after...

Both: ...day after...

Father: ...day after day, I watched and I waited...and I ached in my heart as only a parent can for his child. Most importantly, I never gave up on him. I believed that one day he would return. I just knew it would happen one day.

Son: One day it hit me, and I realized that back at my father's house, his lowliest workers were doing better than I was! They had a place to live; they had food to eat; heck, they were living like kings compared to me. And so I wondered...

Father: *What if he never comes to his senses? What if he doesn't come back? What if I never see him again?*

Son: Again and again I ran things through my head as I made the long journey back to my father's house. I knew what I would do. I would humbly ask him to hire me as one of his workers. I couldn't ask for a handout, and I had no right to ask him to take me back as his son. But maybe he'd let me work for him. Just maybe.

Father: *Maybe today he'll come home* was the thought that ran through my head every day. *Maybe today I'll be sitting here waiting and watching, and I'll see him appear off in the distance as he makes his journey back home.*

Son: "Home." It's a word that describes so many things: comfort, care, security, acceptance, love—and now I was just a few hundred yards away from it.

Father:	It was a beautiful day. I was sitting out on the front porch enjoying a cool breeze when I saw him.
Son:	He stood up out of his chair, looked my direction, and squinted his eyes to get a better look at me. I wondered what he was thinking. I wondered how he felt about me. Would he tell me, "I told you so"?
Father:	I told you so! I told you! I told you he would come back. None of you would listen to me, but I knew…I didn't ever give up on him…I knew.
Son:	I just knew he was going to be angry. The closer I got to the house, the more I knew I'd made the wrong decision. So I stopped…
Father:	He just stood there.
Son:	I couldn't move.
Father:	I couldn't just stand there, so…
Son:	He jumped. He literally jumped off the porch. I'd never seen him do that before. He was like a little kid all excited about something, and then it hit me…he was excited about…me! So what did I do?
Father:	You know what I did next?
Both:	I ran!
Father:	My heart was pounding, and all I could do was run to him.
Son:	I'd never seen him run so fast! His arms stretched out as if to say, "Welcome home."
Father:	"Welcome home!" I shouted, but he was still too far off to hear me. But we kept running; we both kept running toward each other. I just wanted him to jump into my arms like he did when he was a little boy so I could let him know it would be all right. As he got closer, I could see the tears running down his face.
Son:	He was crying…
Father:	Tears of joy! You know what my son did next? He jumped…

Son: I actually jumped! I was so excited, so scared, so...so...so I jumped. And my father...

Father: I caught him. And then...

Son: He hugged me. My father embraced me like only a father can. "I'm so sorry," I told him. "Please forgive me. I don't deserve to be called your son."

Father: My son! My son is back. Bring him some clean clothes, put shoes on his feet. Prepare a meal...no, a *feast*! For my son will no longer live life as an orphan. Today we will celebrate, for all our hopes have come true.

Son: I guess it was hope that kept me going. A hope that my father would have mercy on me. A hope that in some way he would take me back. A hope that I would be forgiven.

Father: Forgiven...it's all forgiven. I'll never bring it up again. There is no blame; there is no anger; there is nothing but joy. For my son was lost, but now he's found.

THE END.

SKIT 3.5

"MY HERO"

BY EDDIE JAMES & TOMMY WOODARD WITH BRIAN CROPP

This true story was told to us at a workshop. We're grateful for it and for the effect it's had on our lives.

WHAT: As he examines a lifetime of gifts given to him by his father, Mike realizes that what his dad actually gave him was all he ever wanted. (Themes: parents, giving, sacrifice, missions, Father's Day, Christmas, remembrance)

WHO: Mike, Dad, Mom

WHEN: Present day

WHY: Matthew 7:9-11; Acts 20:35; Colossians 2:6-7

WEAR: Pajamas, envelope with card, present with sweater, two wedding rings
(COSTUMES AND PROPS)

HOW: Keep the interactions between the family members as natural and light as possible in order to really emphasize the powerful turn at the end of the skit.

Mike addresses the audience.

Mike: I've been thinking over exactly what I wanted to say, y'know, so I wouldn't sound stupid, but I guess that's not gonna happen, so...The greatest thing I ever learned from my dad was about giving. I'm a slow learner, so it's taken me most of my life...but I can remember, I must've been seven years old. It was Christmas morning, and all I'd been hoping for was this stupid action figure. I mean, it seems lame now, but back then, I thought I'd die without it.

Christmas morning. **Mom** *and* **Dad** *enter in pajamas.*

Mom: It's time to open presents.

Mike:	Can I play Santa?
Dad:	Sure.
Mike:	(*Finds present*) It's for me!
Dad:	Open it up.

Mike tears into it.

Mike:	(*Pulls out…*) A sweater?
Mom:	You need some warm things.
Mike:	But I wanted…
Dad:	Hey, don't be ungrateful, Michael. Remember, it's a gift. You didn't earn it. You don't deserve it. Be grateful that you got anything at all.

Mom and *Dad* exit as *Mike* talks to audience.

Mike:	Not exactly what a kid wants to hear on Christmas, but he was right. Then there's my 15th birthday. We're all sitting there. I'm expecting, I dunno, a computer, a car a year early, a hundred bucks, I dunno, but I'm waiting, and my dad hands me this envelope…

Mom and *Dad* enter, still in pajamas.

Dad:	(*Hands over envelope*) Here you go, son.

Mike tears into envelope, excited.

Mike:	(*Holds up a card*) What's this?
Dad:	Well, I got to thinking, and most gifts we get you are kind of meaningless. You either lose interest in them, or they wear out. So we decided to get you something that would have some lasting value.
Mike:	Great! What is it?
Dad:	We sponsored a child for you.

Mom:	From Guatemala.
Mike:	You gave me an orphan kid in South America?
Dad:	No, Mike, we didn't "give you an orphan kid in South America." We gave you the opportunity to do something bigger than yourself. We gave you the ability to make a difference in someone's life! What's his name?
Mike:	(*Reads*) Lupe.
Dad:	Just think, now you have the opportunity to build a relationship with someone in another country. You get to provide hope for Lupe's future. In fact, what we give in your name will help send Lupe to school!
Mike:	This is the most crazyy idea I've ever heard of! (*Addresses audience*) Send him to school? I was trying to get out of school; why would I want to send poor Lupe there? (*Pause*) And then there was that time just a couple of weeks ago. Dad had gone into the hospital, but the rest of us were home on Christmas to open most of the presents. (*Pause*) I got some cool stuff, I guess; I just couldn't help thinking how I'd rather have Dad there with us. (*Pause*) I said something to that effect to Mom, and she told me what happened just after that Christmas when I was seven…

Mom and *Dad* share a moment.

Dad:	You know, he really wants whatever that toy is.
Mom:	But he doesn't have any warm clothes. What he needs is a sweater. He'll grow out of that toy anyway.
Dad:	He'll grow out of the sweater too. (*Pause*) The thing is, we just can't afford to get him anything. I hate this part of Christmas. I want so badly to give him something, but I can't.
Mom:	What are you saying?
Dad:	I'm saying he's my son. I'd give him the world if I could. I'd give him mountains of gold…(*Stops as he sees his wedding ring. He takes it off*) I'd give him gold.
Mom:	Dear?

Dad: Give me yours, too. Mike needs clothes more than toys, so we'll hock these to get them. Besides, my family is more important.

Mike: (*To audience*) So they pawned their wedding rings so I could be warm. I didn't even notice. I just wanted my toy. (*Pause*) Well, since we're all here today to remember Dad, I just thought I should say in front of all of you, my dad was...*is* my hero, because my dad knew that giving was truly better than receiving. Instead of sending flowers, please give money to the scholarship fund we've set up in Dad's name...we're sending Lupe to college.

THE END.

MONOLOGUES  4.0

WHY DO I FEEL SO ALONE?

Umm, yeah...maybe that's because you forgot to shower, or because your personality repels people, or maybe...just maybe, it's because you're doing a monologue.

It's been said, "Every church has at least one good actor." And we're the ones who said it—in our first book, *Instant Skits*. (Yes, that was yet another shameless plug intended to entice you to purchase it!) But back to monologues. We know you've been there—you've looked over the group of people who are willing to do a skit, and you can only see one person you trust to "bring home the bacon." Or you've asked for volunteers to do a skit, and only one person showed up. Worse yet, maybe *no one* showed up, and it's just you, baby!

Well, fear no more, we've got monologues for you. Yes, these powerful little "skits for one" are there to help you out when you feel lonely. Monologues are a great way to get a point across because they have the feel of a testimony. There is a unique connection with the audience that comes inherently with a monologue; it's basically one person looking into the eyes of the audience and telling her story. In essence, the audience members become the other characters in the skit. The truth is, you're not alone with a monologue; there's just nobody standing onstage with you. (Hmm, come to think of it, that's pretty much what *alone* means.)

Monologues can be quite difficult to perform. There's such a fine line between grabbing the attention of the audience and overacting. And finding the balance between wandering the stage and utilizing your space is just as tricky. As the only actor, there's no one for you to cue from—and it's all up to you. Talk about pressure! Just think of yourself as the mythic Highlander and tell yourself, "In the end, there can be only *one*!"

SKIT TIPS

1. **WHO AM I, ANYWAY?** The important thing to remember with a monologue is that this is *not* the time to "be yourself." This is the *character's* moment to shine. As with any skit, the actor needs to take on the physical and verbal characteristics of the person he is portraying. Think about how the person would talk, walk, gesture, and even how he would look at the audience. You may be the only actor onstage, but the audience should be watching the *character*, not you.

2. **DON'T ACT LIKE A CAR SALESMAN ON TV.** Have you ever noticed how the car salesmen on TV overemphasize their gestures and yell at the camera? For some reason, many actors do the same thing with monologues. What makes a monologue easier to watch is when you keep it natural and, if anything, downplay all movement and gestures. There is one exception to this rule: If you want to look like Screech from *Saved by the Bell,* then by all means, overdo it.

3. **GET DRESSED UP AND PROPPED UP.** To help an audience buy into the character you're portraying, monologues are a great opportunity to utilize costumes. Sometimes it could just be a hat or glasses, or you might want to go all out with the full costume regalia. Although many monologues don't require props, some are made more complete with them. Using props also gives the actor something to do with her hands, which just might help her avoid that car-salesman syndrome we were talking about.

4. **BE STILL AND KNOW THAT I AM ACTING.** There's something strange and powerful about silence during a monologue. A silent pause at just the right moment can cause an audience to feel uncomfortable, laugh harder, or empathize with the character. In a similar way, making the choice to stay still instead of moving around can sometimes draw focus better than lots of movement. As an actor, don't be afraid to discover the strength of doing what your parents told you to do when you were a kid: "Shut up and be still!"

5. **MIRROR, MIRROR ON THE WALL, WHO'S THE ACTOR WITH IT ALL?** Before you hit the stage with your monologue, step in front of a mirror and deliver your lines. Even though you'll be the only one onstage, block out any movement you may make. Think about what you're going to do with your hands and facial expressions. We suggest you show your monologue to someone who will be honest with you regarding whether the choices you've made are overdone, boring, or flat.

"LARRY THE LIAR"

BY EDDIE JAMES & TOMMY WOODARD WITH BRIAN CROPP

WHAT: In this monologue, Larry is repeatedly caught in his lies as he recounts how he first came to know about a Christlike love (Themes: honesty, evangelism)

WHO: Larry, Buzzerer

WHEN: Present day

WHY: Proverbs 30:8; Matthew 28:16-19; Ephesians 4:25

WEAR: Bell, buzzer, or some kind of noisemaker
(COSTUMES AND PROPS)

HOW: This skit works best when the person working the buzzer is as familiar with the skit as the actor playing Larry. The timing between these two people is critical to the success of this skit.

Larry stands alone onstage with a very cocky attitude. Offstage is a buzzer ready to catch Larry in his lies.

Larry: Hello. My name's Larry...and I'm an alcoholic. (*Buzz*) I'm an overeater. (*Buzz*) Okay, I'm a liar. But nobody knows it 'cause I'm so good. (*Buzz*) I got skills. (*Buzz*) Okay, everyone knows. But that's not my fault 'cause I was born this way. (*Buzz*) 'Cause I had a rough childhood. (*Buzz*) 'Cause it makes me feel better. Wouldja just let me tell it? Sheesh!

There's this guy at school, they say. I don't know that I could pick him out of a crowd. (*Buzz*) Maybe if I saw his picture. (*Buzz*) Okay, he sits in front of me in English.

Real religious type. Guy can't say two words without mentioning how tight he is with God. So there I am just chillin' with my girl. (*Buzz*) Hangin' with my fellas. (*Buzz*) Okay, I was in home ec. (*Pause*) Don't laugh. I make a mean crème brûlée.

Anyway, I had just ruined a beautiful flan. I don't know what distracted me. (*Buzz*) I don't want to talk about it. (*Buzz*) My dog just died. (*Buzz*) Okay, my parents were splitting up. But it's okay, 'cause everyone knew it was comin'. (*Buzz*) I knew it was comin'. (*Buzz*) Anyway…

Well, I got, y'know, an F on the flan, and I couldn't even find it in me to care. I asked to be excused and went to the bathroom, and that guy's in there. He says to me, "What's wrong?" I figured the guy's a psychic. (*Buzz*) Okay, so maybe I said something. (*Buzz*) Okay, so maybe I was cryin' like a baby. I said, "Nothin's wrong." And he said I was lyin'. Called me a liar right to my face. Can you believe that? (*Pause*)

So I told Mr. Smarty Pants what's goin' on. I told him about my parents, that I got my fourth speeding ticket in a month and I'm about to lose my car, that I was king of the school last week but suddenly I'm nothin' and I have no idea why. (*Buzz*) If I had a book entitled *Why Larry Is No Longer King*, I still wouldn't know. (*Buzz*) If Einstein with all his intelligence explained it to me, I'd have nary a clue. (*Buzz*) If the heavens opened up and the Lord himself gave me a revelation about it, I would still have no idea. (*Buzz*) Okay, I have some idea.

And I was waitin'—waitin' for him to tell me what a mess I was and that if I'd just get my life together—get religion an' all that—then my parents wouldn't split. But he didn't. All he said was, "I'm sorry." He's sorry? What's he got to be sorry for? And then he told me some bad stuff happened to him, and the only thing that got him through it was his relationship with Jesus. Then I smelled something funny, and it wasn't the toilets. (*Looks up to see if the buzzer will go off on the toilet line*)

Anyway, why's this guy tryin' to be my friend all of a sudden? And then it hits me. I don't know why it took me so long, since I *am* a registered genius. (*Buzz*) I have a 3.0 grade point average. (*Buzz*) 2.0? (*Buzz*) Okay, never mind, but I got street smarts. (*Long buzz*) Wouldja lay off that thing?

Okay, so it dawns on me, he's not trying to con anybody; he thinks he's telling the truth. Strange thing to be standin' in the presence of the insane.

But I rose above it. I didn't want anything to do with this God stuff. (*Buzz*) I said I could see where he was comin' from, but that it didn't change anything. (*Buzz*) All right, I might've given it some thought. But I think I was, y'know, I was caught up in my emotions or somethin'. (*Buzz*) Weak stomach? (*Buzz*) Knock it off. So what if it spoke right to me? That doesn't change anything. (*Buzz*) No, it doesn't. (*Buzz*) Quit it! It didn't affect me. (*Buzz*) Why are you doing this to me? I asked him to pray for me—no big deal. (*Buzz*) Look, I'm…(*Buzz*) I haven't done…(*Buzz*) You want me to say it changed me? Well, it didn't. (*Buzz*) It didn't! (*Buzz*) Okay, it changed me!

Pause. No buzz.

That's the truth. Y'know, I guess my little conversation with that guy showed me I was more open to a relationship with God than I thought.

Well, I have to go. I've got…a hot date. (*Pause. Starts to walk off. Buzz*) To work in a homeless shelter. (*Buzz*) To be a missionary to India. (*Buzz*) To work for the Salvation Army? (*Buzz*) My grandmother's sick? (*Buzz*) Okay, I've got a crème brûlée in the oven. Bye. (*Exits*)

THE END.

"THE VEIL"

BY EDDIE JAMES & TOMMY WOODARD WITH TED & NANCIE LOWE

What: Moments before her wedding, a young bride reveals the heartache she suffers over her decision not to save herself until marriage. (Themes: love, sex, dating, consequences)

Who: Stephanie

When: Present day

Why: Psalm 119:9; Matthew 5:27-28; 1 Corinthians 6:13

Wear:
(COSTUMES
AND PROPS)   Wedding veil, wedding dress (It's okay if a wedding dress can't be found, but the veil is critical.)

How: This drama can be very powerful if the actress truly knows her lines and is able to deliver them with confidence. The correct tone and expression are critical for this sketch to be interesting and understandable, but the impact makes it worth the effort.

---

*As the scene opens, **Stephanie**, wearing her wedding veil, anxiously awaits the music that will begin her wedding.*

Stephanie: How does it look? It has to be perfect because today is supposed to be the most special day of my life. (*She takes off the veil*) Today, I will walk down the aisle with my father, and he will give me away. My best friends will show their love for me by wearing the ugliest dresses in the world. Then Robby and I will say our vows and be presented as husband and wife.

    And then there will be the reception, which I am a little worried about because the music will be provided by my brother's garage band, "Black Death." Robby and I will cram cake into each other's faces. (*Demonstrates, and laughs*) I used to think that that was the most pathetic thing I'd ever seen, but today the thought of feeding him cake seems, well…precious.

Then, we'll dance and stare into each other's eyes. We'll laugh as we dash to the car in a shower of bubbles. (*Pause*) Yes, bubbles because rice makes birds' tummies, well...explode. Then we'll leave in my car, which I'm sure Robby's brothers will decorate with shaving cream, tin cans, and lewd remarks written in shoe polish.

Today is supposed to be the most perfect day. (*She changes her tone, nervous and almost teary*) But today, instead of feeling giddy, I feel insecure. Today, instead of having butterflies in my stomach, I feel sick.

Not sick about today, I'm sick about tonight. You know, the "wedding night." Tonight is supposed to be the most tender, romantic night ever. But you see, I think I've made it less special—no, I *know* I've made it less special. Because I chose not to wait.

Holding the veil to her waist as if it were a dress, she continues.

You know, as I look in the mirror and see myself in this white dress, I have to ask myself—as painful as it may be, I have to ask myself—*Why didn't I save myself for this day? Was it because my dad wasn't affectionate with me?* I recently heard a speaker say, "Dads, if you are not affectionate with your daughter, then there's a guy out there who will be more than willing to show her that affection." So was that it? Was that my problem? Did my dad not hug me enough? Maybe, but any way you look at it, I still made the choice—the wrong choice.

When I was in high school, there didn't seem to be a choice. Everyone had sex; you were supposed to have sex, right? Everybody was sexually active in some way. Sleeping with your boyfriend was totally acceptable. In fact, it was encouraged. Don't get me wrong, there was a *huge* difference between sleeping around and sleeping with your boyfriend...well, at least that's what I thought.

When I think about that first time, I don't think I planned to do it...or even really wanted to. It just happened, and I didn't try to stop it. I mean, after all, he was my boyfriend—he took me out on dates; he called me; he talked to me at school; and he liked me a lot, right?

But I had one friend, Amanda, and she was different. She didn't buy into that. I remember one time I just asked her, "Amanda, how do you wait? Why do you wait?" And she said without the slightest hesitation, "God has created us to love only one person in that way. I want to give my future husband all of me."

I'll never forget that day. What Amanda said hit me so hard; and even though everybody else said the opposite, I knew Amanda was right. I even went so far as to tell my boyfriend that I wanted to stop. But how do you stop? I mean, how do you go back to just holding hands? I had always heard "wait," but no one told me how to stop once I'd started. I finally just gave up; after all, I'd done it before—I had crossed the line; I had jumped the fence; there was no going back. It wasn't as if I were "sleeping around"; I mean, they were all my boyfriends, right?

To be honest, I just basically convinced myself that it was no big deal. I mean, I never got pregnant. I never got any kind of disease. I didn't wait…but that was okay, right? Then I met Robby. Robby is my fiancé. We met about two years ago. He's great. He has sandy blond hair, blue eyes, and the most beautiful smile you've ever seen. And the way he makes me laugh—I never knew I could laugh so much.

Best of all, he loves Jesus. And he loves me; I know that. How do I know that? He loves me so much, he told me we should wait until we get married to have sex. It's ironic: I found out it takes more love to say *no* than it does to say *yes*.

(*Excited again*) I love Robby. I am going to spend the rest of my life with him, and tonight is our wedding night—and I'm scared. I once heard this thing about "sexual ghosts"—memories of people you slept with that float through your mind while you're in bed with your husband. I don't know if it's just a myth to scare people into virginity or if it's the honest truth. I guess I'll find out tonight.

I love Robby; I would do anything for him. Most of all, I wish I could take back the choices I made with other guys. He deserves better than that. I deserve better than that. I wish I could give my husband all of me, but tonight he will only get a part of me—because there are things I chose to give away before tonight.

Oh, don't get me wrong; I know I've been forgiven. I mean, Robby and I talked about it. I can't tell you the number of times I've prayed about it. So I know it's forgiven. However, *forgiveness* is one thing; *forgetting* it is another. I wish I could forget it. I wish I could go back in time and change it all. I wish…(*long pause*) well, it doesn't matter what I wish.

Well, I'd better finish getting ready (*puts the veil back on her head, but not covering her face*)—after all, I'm about to walk down the aisle. Today is going to be the happiest day of my life, right?

THE END.

"THE BIG PICTURE"
BY EDDIE JAMES & TOMMY WOODARD WITH CHARISSA FISHBECK

WHAT: Using a flashlight as a tool, a teenager explains the incredible difference it can make to look at ourselves through God's eyes instead of our own. (Themes: self-esteem, new creation, God's love, grace, forgiveness)

WHO: Teenager (guy or girl)

WHEN: Present day

WHY: Psalm 139:14; John 8:12; 2 Corinthians 5:17

WEAR: Working flashlight
(COSTUMES AND PROPS)

HOW: This is a long monologue. Memorize it in chunks. If it seems too long, take out some of the words without messing up the point. The more it feels as if the actor is talking to the audience "naturally," the better this monologue will take off.

The stage is in total darkness as **Teenager** *enters, with the only light showing from the flashlight in* **Teenager's** *hand.*

Teenager: Hey! What happened to the lights? Hello? Is anyone out there? Anyone? Hang on, I think I found the switch. (*Stage lights come up to show actor upstage with his back to the audience*) There we go, that's better. (*Turns around, sees audience, and says, surprised*) Hey…good to…see ya. We had a…light problem…of some kind…lights wouldn't work. Lucky for me…I had a flashlight handy.

Good old flashlight. I've always loved flashlights. I mean, what's not to love? Stranded on a desert island, SOS with your flashlight. (*Flicks flashlight in mock Morse Code*) Bored in your room at night—hello, laser light show. Practicing to be the next American Idol…(*Singing into the flashlight like a microphone*) Thank you, Mr. Flashlight. Need a special effect for your ghost story? (*Shines flashlight under face*) The flashlight of fear! Need to knock someone out? These little guys will do the job. (*Pause*) Um… forget that last one. That's a little harsh. You know, come to think of it, I'm just a flashlight kind of person.

Not because I enjoy being in the dark. Trust me, I slept with my closet light on until I was…well, actually I still do. And no, I'm not a big camping enthusiast, either. My idea of camping is staying at a cheap hotel. I guess I feel like a flashlight person because I like to see things one step, or one part, at a time.

You've heard that saying—we all have—that God doesn't give us flood-lights so we can see every little thing going on in our lives at once. Instead, God gives us *flashlights* to show us the very next step we're supposed to take, and nothing more. We've all heard that saying, right? (*Pause*)

Well, I've heard it. Anyway, that used to really annoy me because I wished God would just go ahead and show me the whole thing so it would all just make sense. The *big picture*, I would say; show me the *big picture*. Let me see how it all works together so I can trust that you know what you're doing.

Not anymore. The big picture absolutely terrifies me. The more I see, the more I understand; the more I know, the more scared I am. And if I'm not careful, the smaller God becomes. I've learned that the more this world makes sense to me—the more I understand what's going on in my life—the less I'm allowing God to be as big as God really is. Because believe me, a world that I can explain is not a world God made. I know now that if God were to turn those floodlights on, it would completely blow my mind. No thanks, Lord. Just gimme my flashlight back, hold my hand, and we'll be fine. I've decided I don't want to be you after all. (*Pause*)

I think being a "flashlight" person is cool, but my problem is, I've gotten a little too good at pointing that flashlight around, especially when I look at myself. (*Turns flashlight back on, points it at heart*) I can be pretty cruel with my little light, shining it right on my guilt, my faults, and my flaws. With my trusty flashlight, I can send a laser beam backward across time to find the perfect memory of the moments I fell flat on my face, made a horrible decision, or failed miserably to please God. Sometimes, when I look at myself with my flashlight, all I can see is ugliness and failure, surrounded by darkness and shadow. (*Holds flashlight under face again, sadly*)

(*Turns flashlight off, looks up*) But the good news is, that's not how God looks at me. You see, God can handle seeing the big picture because he's the one who made it. Look at it like this: Have you ever really looked at the mountains? I mean, *really* looked? Think about it—there's no reason for a mountain range to be as beautiful as it is. It's just made of rocks, bushes, weeds, and dirt. But take a few steps back, let God turn some creative light on—and that combination of rocks, bushes, weeds, and dirt becomes an amazing view arranged by a Master Artist. Not in a million years could I, or anybody else, create such beauty and such power out of such pitiful ingredients.

You know, if our God can make something beautiful with nothing but rocks and dirt, think of what God can do with us. All we have to do is put ourselves in God's hands, allow *God's* light to shine on us, take a step or two back, and look at the big picture.

Can you believe it? That you can be beautiful? That I can be beautiful? After a while, that's something we all just stop hoping for. I mean, I know myself—just look at all the nasty things I can find with my little flashlight. It's a long list of sins, mistakes, and bad memories. There was a time when I was pretty much convinced that I'd seen all there was of me, and none of it was any good, much less "beautiful."

But until I took a good look at those mountains, I had forgotten: I'm a creation of that Master Artist too. And even though I've produced a lot of rocks, bushes, weeds, and dirt, the same God who made each and every mountain range also created *me.* God can take years of mistakes, an imperfect body, a mind full of dark thoughts, and an unfaithful heart—and shape it all into something more than worthwhile—something amazing. All I've got to do is take that flashlight and point it where it belongs—to the path in front of me—and let God take care of the rest.

Wow! That was a lot from just being lost in the dark. But isn't that just like God? Take someone who is lost in the dark, shine a little light on him, and do something amazing.

THE END.

"WELCOME BACK, LAZARUS"
BY EDDIE JAMES & TOMMY WOODARD

MONOLOGUE

4.4

WHAT: A firsthand account of one of Jesus' most amazing miracles, told from Lazarus' perspective. (Themes: miracles, healing, power over death, faith, witnessing)

WHO: Lazarus

WHEN: Bible times

WHY: Isaiah 55:9; Luke 1:37; John 11:1-44

WEAR:
(COSTUMES AND PROPS)

Lazarus should be wrapped in a material that will appear to be burial clothes while still allowing the actor to move. You may even want to wrap him up like a mummy to the point that he has to hop onstage. But make sure he can at least move his upper body and arms.

HOW: Energy is the key with this monologue. Make good eye contact with the audience to really draw them in. You may even want to give Lazarus some kind of accent. Read the account of this miracle in the Bible before you begin this skit.

---

*As the scene opens, **Lazarus** enters, still wrapped in his burial clothes, dazed by what he has just experienced.*

Lazarus: *(Enters halfway in…stops…looks confused…looks back at where he came from…looks back toward center stage…pauses…slowly moves forward to center stage…pauses…looks out at audience)* Can you see me? I mean, I'm really here, right? 'Cause…I'm…not…sure…what just happened. *(Long pause)* I just woke up in a tomb. *(Pause)* HELLO! A TOMB! You know…RIP…the final resting place…"Days Inn" for the dead. Can you imagine?

I know, I know—you think I'm crazy. I would too. But I'm not…I don't think.

Wait…let me back up. Okay, I got sick one day—nothing big—just a little upset stomach. I just figured I'd eaten a bad chalupa or something. So my stomach was hurting, and I was a little more gassy than usual. It seemed like no big deal at first, but then this thing wouldn't go away. It got worse. So I took some Pepcid; I took some Pepto—nothing worked. I asked my sister Mary to pray for me. She's such a great pray-er; however, she ain't so good at keeping a secret. She blabbed to my other sister, Martha, that I was sick. Martha, God bless her, is a bit of a busybody. She's always trying to "help" people. Translation: she's bossy and she thinks she knows what everybody else should be doing. I started burning up—to feel like stale rye—which isn't a good thing at all.

A day later, I couldn't get out of bed! I don't know what it was, but every time I got out of bed, I felt like I was being punched in the gut. So now I was getting a little worried, wondering what the heck was wrong with me. Martha was running around the house going, "Try this, eat this, drink this!" Mary was at the foot of my bed praying, "Please don't let him die; please don't let him die." What a prayer! She was freaking me out! I mean, I thought I *was* going to die after all those weird prayers! (*Chuckles…then thinks about it*) Hmm…well, I guess I was.

Then all of a sudden I got this thought: *I wish Jesus were here.* He's a family friend; we always love it when he comes over. Life can be crazy, but when Jesus comes over, it all calms down. So I said out loud, "If Jesus were here, I bet I'd feel better."

Well, that put the sisters into overdrive. Mary started praying, "Lord, send your Son. Send Jesus." At one point, she actually put her fingers on her temples and started acting like she was talking to him via telekinesis. (*Puts fingers on temples and mocks* **Mary**) "Come in, Jesus. Jesus, come in. Do you read me? This is Foot Washer, calling Son of Man…come in, Son of Man…do you read me?" Martha, on the other hand, started shouting at people, "Do you know where Jesus is? Can any of you help me find Jesus? You, why are you just standing there? Go find Jesus. Mary, don't just kneel there…go get Jesus!"

I just knew Jesus would come. It even made me feel a little better just thinking about it. But a day went by…no Jesus…but I knew he would come. Another day…no Jesus, and I was getting worse…but I knew he would come…I just knew it. My sisters were talking to each other: "Where is he? This is not like him. Why isn't he here?" But I just assured them, "Don't worry. He'll come. He's our friend. He loves and cares for us. Oh, he'll come."

Meanwhile, I started to fade in and out. I was having great conversations with my Uncle Samuel. This may not sound like a big deal to you, but it was for me—he died about 10 years ago! (*Pauses for a moment, makes freaked-out face, and shivers, as if creeped out*) Creepy, ain't it? However, I have to admit he looked pretty good—for a dead guy.

So anyway, day three, and still no Jesus. Now I was talking to other people who had "gone before me": my Aunt Rebecca, my Grandpa Joe—and they were saying things like, "Hey, Laz, you can come to our place tomorrow," which, I thought, sounded pretty good. Meanwhile, my sisters were beside themselves. I kept asking them, "Why are you crying? There's Uncle Samuel, and he looks great!" That didn't seem to help, so I reassured them one more time, "Don't worry; he'll come." Then, it started to get very dark…and…like you've heard before…there was this bright light…

The next thing I knew, I heard someone calling my name: "Lazarus! Come out!" I was groggy. You know how you feel right after you've slept a few hours too long…or a few days too long? And I didn't want to wake up for some reason. It was like I was having this really great dream and I didn't want it to end. My eyes were still closed, and I was thinking to myself, *That voice, I know that voice.* And then I realized it: He came. I knew he would. He always does.

I opened my eyes, expecting to see Mary at my feet and maybe smell some of Martha's cooking. But…I…didn't. Instead, I saw Uncle Samuel… or what's left of him, wrapped in this stuff (*holds up his burial clothes*), and I smelled…something rotten. I mean, it was awful. Then I had the worst revelation of my life: *That smell is me!* Needless to say, I freaked out. I struggled to get to my feet and began to hop out of this tomb, desperately trying to get away from my dead uncle and my own smell.

As I hopped out, I saw this crowd of people all staring at me. No one moved a muscle. They weren't smiling. They weren't crying. They all just had this blank look on their faces like they'd just seen a ghost. Awwwwkward! Then I realized…I'm the ghost! I hopped over to the only person in the group who was smiling at this point: Jesus.

Have you ever seen Jesus smile? It is, by far, the greatest sight in the universe. He was smiling at me with tear-stained cheeks. I'd never seen him cry before, and he wasn't crying now—but he had been. He looked at me and then he leaned forward and whispered in my ear, "Welcome back, friend." That's when it really hit me. So here I am now, trying to sort it all out. I still don't understand it all, but just talking to you seems to have helped. So, thanks so much for listening; I was dying to talk to someone about it.

THE END.

"GRADUATION DAY"
BY EDDIE JAMES & TOMMY WOODARD

WHAT: At a high school graduation, an unlikely speaker shares his off-kilter philosophies and unloads his opinions on his unsuspecting classmates. (Themes: the future, relationships, fear, God's calling)

WHO: Rodney, Principal Dithers

WHEN: Present day

WHY: Psalm 16:5; Psalm 90:12; Proverbs 24:14

WEAR:
(COSTUMES
AND PROPS)
If possible, a graduation cap and gown would be a great addition to this skit. Also, Rodney needs a piece of paper from which to read his "speech."

HOW: Although this is a monologue, it would be great to have someone come out as the school principal in the beginning. It will add to the effectiveness of the speech. You could also choose to allow the principal character to remain offstage and just use a microphone.

Principal Dithers: Welcome to the graduation ceremony for the Edison High School class of *(insert current year)*. As your principal, it is, unfortunately, my duty to inform you that no one had a high enough GPA to qualify as a state-recognized valedictorian. Therefore, to determine who would give the graduation speech, we placed all the "most likely to" winners in a hat and drew one. The winner of the graduation speech lotto, and the person who will give our graduation speech this year, is the class of *(insert current year)* student who was voted "most likely to moon the principal"—Rodney Edginton.

Rodney enters, wearing cap and gown.

Rodney: Heyyyyy, everybody! Waazzz upppp? Wow, who would have thunk that I would be giving the main graduation speech? It was so cool: I got this call last night, so I'm ready to parlay words of wisdom into your souls. First off, to the board of education, Principal Dithers, Vice Principal Dinkston, all the teachers, coaches, and other adults at the school who I have never been able to figure out what you actually do...to all of you, on behalf of the graduating class of (*insert current year*), I say *thank you* for your hours of toil as you have worked to instill in us that which we know as education.

To the parents, siblings, grandparents, uncles, aunts, cousins, close friends, and other friends who could not come up with a good excuse to get out of attending this boring ceremony...to all of you, I also say thank you on behalf of the graduating class of (*insert current year*) for your wonderful support and unending encouragement throughout the years. We're better people for it. Thanks, also, because we're still going to hit you up for more money as a lot of us go off to college to trek through another four years of education before finding gainful employment, or as we squander most of our twenty-something years away sitting at Starbucks and philosophizing about what a "real" job would look like.

Man! This is so cool getting to do this. I feel so stinkin' important!

(*Regains composure as if to make a serious speech*) To the class of (*insert current year*), my classmates, my friends, my school "family"...I say to you: Congratulations! We finally made it. Well, at least most of us did. Sorry, Bubba. You tried. Maybe next year...again.

I think someone famous, or almost famous, once said...and I quote... "We stand today at a crossroads in life that inevitably will take us somewhere." I think someone said that because that is what roads do: They take us places. To this, I must add that it is you, and only you, and you alone, who will determine who you will be and what you will do for the rest of your life. Do not follow where the path may lead; go instead where there is no path and leave a trail. But cover your trail in a way that will protect you and your trail from those who would seek to rob you of that which is yours and what you determine you will be and what you will do for the rest of your life...because it is you, and only you, and you alone, who determines this as you come to a fork in the road...a fork you and I must take, because life is full of forks, spoons, and knives trying to cut us off at the knees. Don't let them take away the trails, paths, and destinies that are about to be laid before us. Say "no" to that evil cutlery and, "yes"—to the spork.

We need to be reminded that we have developed great relationships over the past 12 years. Relationships can be powerful things. They can emancipate us from the oppressive, uncontrollable facts of life. They embolden us, enabling us to accept our condition and allowing us to move on to newer friendships, never forgetting the bonds that bind.

The insane, alone man has no sense of reality, but the man with friends has in his possession a rational, realistic view of the world. The insane, alone man speaks to the air and makes no sense, but the sane man with friends makes the air make sense. The insane, alone man says, "Man the battle stations, for the spaghetti king is dancing sideways in a rain hat and galoshes," but the man with friends keeps his insane thoughts to himself. That is the power of friendship. Looking out into your eyes, I can see you know what I mean.

I wish I had the time to speak to each one of you, but that would take way too long; and my grandmother, who came all the way from Boise, would fall asleep. I just know this: Most of us will meet up at our five-, 10-, and 20-year reunions. So, allow me to share some wisdom with you. Even though I may not mention your name, that doesn't mean you don't need to take a long, hard look in the mirror.

First off: Brian Upshaw. For the past 12 years, you have griped about being overweight, yet you have eaten super nachos at lunch every day? Holy cow, you probably have a bag of chips under your graduation gown right now, don't you? (*Pause*) See, I told you. Get a clue, Brian. Put the chips down.

Cindy Tinsley. Do you really think you can drink like a fish every weekend and still be president of Students Against Alcohol and Drugs? I'm sorry, but that really is just so SAAD. Not to mention making a lot of our moms MADD.

Allison Billington. If you think you're too hot for me, why didn't you get a date to prom this year? (*Says under breath, but so that everyone can still hear*) Gosh, that felt so good!

Michael Hutton. Thank you so much for the weekly wedgie you've given me since the seventh grade. As you progress in life, you'll want to reevaluate your method of trying to feel better about yourself, alrighty? Seek counseling, Mikey, and for goodness' sake—make a mental note—no one thinks it's cool when you peel out in the parking lot.

Todd Dexter. Since our freshman year, you've been sporting the unconscious mullet. It's time someone spoke up and told you, "Todd, my boy, you've got a mullet on your head; get that thing cut." (*Looks out*) And looking at the rest of your family today, I want to urge you to encourage them to do the same. Especially your grandpa…(*Looks closer*) Oh, sorry, your grandma.

In closing, may I add, it has been said, "May we never live life like a karaoke singer—using others' words, rhythms, and rhyme—but may we be like Barry Manilow and write the songs that make the whole world sing."

Last but not least, I'll point the mirror at myself. The whole world is an oyster, and we are allowed to partake of this rare pearl—and I am so scared. Scared to death that I may not measure up or find my calling or purpose. Scared to death that I may make a mistake that would stick me in a rut that I can't get out of for the next 20 years. No offense, Dad. Most of all, I'm scared to death that I may waste my life and never figure out what God has called me to do. Wow, I didn't see that coming.

Well…peace out, everybody. (*Starts to walk off, then stops*) Well, I don't want to disappoint everyone, so finally, this is for Principal Dithers. (*Steps to the side of the podium and lifts up his gown as if he is going to moon the audience*)

Principal Dithers: (*From offstage*) No, Rodney!

Lights black out immediately.

ALTERNATE ENDING: Principal Dithers comes running from offstage and tackles Rodney…then lights out.

THE END.

DUETS & ENSEMBLES

5.0

WHERE TWO OR MORE ARE GATHERED

By the way, what do you call a bunch of skit people gathered in one place? A team? A group? A gaggle? A posse? A band? A mob? A company? A troupe? We call them, "A bunch of skitiots"!

Putting together an ensemble piece is like trying to stack up dominoes: When you get it right and have the right balance, it's awesome. But setting it all up takes a lot of time, effort, and patience. And if one thing gets out of line, the whole thing can fall apart quickly. Unlike dominoes, though, when you're tired of working with your actors, you can't put them back in a box and shove them in a drawer. Well, we guess you could, but we're pretty sure you'd get in trouble for it.

Ensemble skits are great because they provide the opportunity to bring in different types of characters. In a monologue you have to describe a scene; in an ensemble piece, you can act it out so people can see it happen. The key to a great ensemble piece is teamwork. Like anyone else, actors can be selfish and want to bask in the spotlight. (There may not be an I in "team," but many actors will point out that there is an M and an E.) However, great ensemble skits require all participants to consider themselves equal, no matter how many lines they may have. There is no room for a "star" in an ensemble piece.

We would encourage you to begin with a small ensemble, otherwise known as a "duet." The world loves great duets: Abbott and Costello, Butch Cassidy and the Sundance Kid, Sonny and Cher—okay, maybe not all of them. Duets provide the benefits of ensemble skits with the ease of working with just two people, but pay attention to the chemistry in your duets. Your two actors need to be able to work together and connect onstage in such a way that it engages the audience and makes them believe what's going on.

These ensemble and duet skits will take a little more rehearsal time, but the reward is worth it. More people onstage means more students getting the opportunity to use their gifts and talents in serving God.

SKIT TIPS

1. **"P" IS FOR PROJECTION.** Although projection is important in all the types of skits in this book, it's most important in ensemble pieces. Why? Because rarely do you find a venue or stage that has enough wireless mics for everyone involved in the skit. Therefore, it's important to make sure your actors can be heard and understood. If one person isn't heard in your ensemble, then the entire skit can be lost. That's a lot of pressure for your "mumbler" kids.

2. **"P" IS FOR PLACEMENT.** Staging is crucial in an ensemble piece. First, make sure you have ample room to perform. Then, block your piece so everyone can be seen and heard all throughout the skit. Take the time to move people around and find the best spots for them to stand so they don't have to turn their backs to the audience. It can get crowded very quickly, if you're not careful. And for goodness sake, try to be creative—don't make your actors stand in a straight line. Use different levels, such as having some actors positioned on furniture, some sitting on the ground, and some standing.

3. **"P" IS FOR PROPS.** Frequently in an ensemble piece, people will need to hand things to each other. Make sure you have secured your props far enough in advance to allow your actors a few rehearsals with them. Also, if you're pantomiming your objects instead of actually using props, it's easy for the skit to slide toward "corny," so have your actors really practice with their imaginary props to make sure they're conveying the item accurately.

4. **"P" IS FOR PAYING ATTENTION.** With multiple people on the stage and multiple things going on, it's very easy for an actor to lose her place or forget her lines. So listen up, actors—the key is to *pay attention* to what's going on. Listen to each other. Interact like your character would. If you're offstage, don't goof off. Stand in the wings and watch what's going on. And always be prepared to step back onstage. It's so tempting to drop character while you're not the focus of the action. So keep this in mind: "If you're *on,* then you're *in.*" Simply stated, this means that if you're somewhere on the stage, then you're still in character. No exceptions. So pay attention, or your whole group will pay for it.

5. **"P" IS FOR COSTUMES.** Yeah, yeah, we know. But what did you want us to say? "P" is for "Play Clothes"? (Darn, you're right—that would have worked.) Anyway, costumes can play a big role in helping your audience buy into your ensemble skit. The more people you have onstage, the easier it is for your audience to get lost in knowing who's who. Even if your costuming is simple and small, do something to help differentiate between the characters.

"BEANIE WEENIES"

BY EDDIE JAMES & TOMMY WOODARD

WHAT: When it comes to witnessing, God can use anyone, and any situation, to tell others about Jesus. (Themes: testimony, witnessing, friends)

WHO: Candace, Stephie

WHEN: Present day

WHY: John 15:5-17; James 2:23

WEAR: None

(COSTUMES AND PROPS)

HOW: This is a fun skit, so play it to the hilt! The bigger you play the "valley girl" aspects of Candace and Stephie in the beginning, the more powerful the serious turn at the end will be.

The skit begins as **Stephie** *addresses the audience to tell her story.*

Stephie: Hi, my name is Stephie (**Candace** *is sneaking up behind her*), and I'm going to tell you my story. Well, see, there's my friend Candace...

Candace: Hi, I'm Candace.

Stephie: (*Shocked—in a good way*) What are you doing here? Oh my gosh, this is so great!

Candace: Well, I'm Candace, and this is Stephie.

Both: And we are *Days of our Lives*-aholics.

Candace:	It's totally our favorite show. We always get *way* too involved in how _____ is cheating on _____, and why he just won't admit he has feelings for _____ .

(Add in current characters from Days of our Lives, or substitute another soap opera)

Stephie:	Anyhoo. Me and Candace always TiVo *Days* and go over to each other's houses after school to watch it.
Candace:	Okay. So, the other day Stephie comes up to my locker and asks me if I want to come over and watch *Days*. And I said, okay.
Stephie:	And I said, okay.
Candace:	And I said, okay.
Stephie:	And I said, okay.
Both:	And we said, okay, okay, okay.
Stephie:	So we're over at my house, and we both get really hungry.
Candace:	Yeah. My stomach was, like, totally growling, so I asked her if she wanted to find something to eat.
Stephie:	And I said, okay.
Candace:	And I said, okay.
Stephie:	And I said, okay.
Candace:	And I said, okay.
Both:	And we said, okay, okay, okay.
Stephie:	We're looking around for some grub, and there is, like, *nothing* to eat. I mean, like, Old Mother Hubbard, the cupboard was bare.
Candace:	Finally, Stephie found a can of Beanie Weenies. She's all trying to get me to eat them, and I'm all, like, "Beanie Weenies?" Sounds so gross. I mean, beans and weenies in a can?

Stephie:	Anyhoo, she finally agreed to eat them, so we nuked them in the micro-wave, and we both sat down to finish watching *Days*. And in walks my brother, Brad—the Brat.
Candace:	And he's all, like, freaking out, yelling, "You're eating my Beanie Weenies! You're eating my Beanie Weenies!"
Stephie:	My brother looked like such a dork going on and on about his Beanie Weenies, and then Candace did something so disgusting...

Stephie takes a step away from Candace.

Candace:	(*To Stephie*) That was totally not my fault at all, and you know that. (*To audience, grossed out at the memory*) I was just laughing so hard that I...that I...shot a beanie right out of my nose.
Stephie:	Brad and I were just standing there looking at her, like, in total shock. And she's got this Beanie juice running down her face.
Candace:	Yeah. (*Points to her backside*) And if you think it smells bad coming outta here...(*points to nose*) you should try it outta here.
Stephie:	Eeeewwww! (*Disgusted*)
Candace:	Anyhoo. (*Rolling eyes at Stephie*) So naturally I excuse myself to the bath-room to blow the beanies out of my nose. And while I'm there, I hear a car pull up.
Stephie:	It was my boyfriend. Kirk.
Candace:	The Jerk. (*To Stephie*) I mean, he's always telling you you're not all that, and he's all this, and you better do what he says. (*To audience*) Stephie totally knows how I feel about their relationship. And even though I never push my thoughts on her, I just always tell her I'm there for her, and I'm praying for her.
Stephie:	So, Candace was in there for quite a while. But then she kinda stuck her head out the door and gave me the "Beanies gone" sign, and Kirk and I went outside.

Candace:	I just sat back down on the couch to wait. Then I saw the bowl of Beanie Weenies, and I thought, *I don't think so*, and set them aside. Finally, Stephie came back in, and you could tell she'd been crying.
Stephie:	So, I looked right at Candace, with my mascara all running, and said, "Candace, tell me about Jesus."
Candace:	I *totally* wasn't expecting that! But I pulled myself together, gave her a tissue and the mascara out of my purse, and said that he was this guy who lived a long time ago, and he wore long robes and Huarache sandals...
Stephie:	And I said, "No. Sirrus?" (*i.e., "Serious"*)
Candace:	And I said, "Sirrus."
Stephie:	Sirrus.
Candace:	So I told her everything I knew about Jesus. And I asked her if she wanted to become a Christian.
Stephie:	I said no. I mean, I just wasn't ready yet, and I really didn't understand what it all meant. Besides, my mascara made me look like a reject from a metal band. I mean, who's going to talk to Jesus looking like that?
Candace:	(*Takes finger down the side of her face as if it were a tear*) I was like, "Tear."
Stephie:	Well, anyhoo, next day at school I ran up to Candace and said, "Guess what?"
Candace:	And I was like, "What?"
Stephie:	And I was like, "Guess what?"
Candace:	And I was like, "What?"
Stephie:	And I was like, "Guess what?"
Candace:	And I said, "Shut up and just tell me."

Stephie: And I looked her right in the eye and told her, "Last night I was in my room, and I prayed. I told God I wanted to follow Jesus! I mean, it was so great! Before I went to sleep that night, I was praying and I was like, "God, I just wanted you to know that you can use me any way you choose. I want to be, like, open and available to do whatever." And God said, "Okay," and I said, "Okay," and we said, "Okay, okay, okay." And then I said, "P.S. God? Next time, can we leave out the Beanie Weenies?"

Both: Bye!

Stephie: We gotta go watch *Days*! (*Both exit*)

THE END.

DUET

5.2

"HEAVENLY DADDY"

BY EDDIE JAMES & TOMMY WOODARD WITH TED & NANCIE LOWE

WHAT: As two children compare their daddies, they demonstrate that although our earthly fathers may not be all we need them to be, our Heavenly Father will never let us down. (Themes: salvation, God as Father)

WHO: Becky, Timmy

WHEN: Present day

WHY: Psalm 68:5; Romans 8:15; Galatians 4:6

WEAR: Barbie™ and Ken™ dolls

(COSTUMES AND PROPS)

HOW: This skit is a lot of fun, but don't overplay the children's characters or they won't be believable. Take extra care to deal gently with the powerful moment when the children talk about our "Heavenly Daddy."

---

*Becky sits by herself, playing with Barbie and Ken who are "talking" to each other. **Timmy** enters.*

Becky: (*In doll voices*) You are so pretty and you are so sweet. Well, *you* are so pretty and *you* are so sweet.

Timmy: Why are you always playing with those dumb old dolls?

Becky: Because I like my Barbies. Why are you always trying to set little kitty cats on fire?

Timmy: Because they're from the devil. And because it's funny. Can I play with one of those dolls?

Becky: No—you'll just rip its head off, throw it in the garbage, and run far, far away. Anyway, my mommy said that you are not allowed to play with my toys anymore.

Timmy:	Well, my mom said you are the devil.
Becky:	(*Crying*) I am *not* the devil! Timmy, you better say you're sorry.
Timmy:	I'm sorry. But can I please play with that Power Ranger in that sparkly bathing suit?
Becky:	He is not a Power Ranger; he is Malibu Daddy.
Timmy:	Can I play with (*sarcastically*) *Malibu Daddy* then?
Becky:	Yes, as long as you promise not to shoot things at Big Pretty Hair Barbie… (*pause*) and we have to play family.
Timmy:	Family, yuck! When my mommy makes us have family time, that means I'm not allowed to watch TV.
Becky:	One time, we had family time, and I had to tell my little brother that I like him—but I don't. Hold on, Barbie has to tell me something. (*Holds Barbie to her ear*) Before we start to play, Barbie said she has to go to the bathroom.
Timmy:	Can't you just tell rubber-head Barbie to hold it?
Becky:	Oh no, she can't hold it because my mommy told me not to hold it. She said if you hold it you could get a kidney *confection*.
Timmy:	I don't have to worry about holding it because I have special pants.
Becky:	Timmy, you are so weird. Now let's play family. (*Gives **Timmy** the Ken doll*)
Timmy:	All right, all right. This is the daddy doll. Every night my daddy gets on his knees by my bed and prays, "Dear God, thank you for Timmy."
Becky:	Why?
Timmy:	Because my daddy loves me more than your daddy loves you.
Becky:	Well, my daddy took God to lunch, and God told my daddy…and then my daddy told God…well, I don't remember everything they said.

Timmy:	How do you know your daddy took God to lunch, if your daddy doesn't even live at your house?
Becky:	Well, my daddy calls me sometimes and tells me stuff—and he sent me these Barbies. And he promised me that if I was a really good girl, then he would take me to Disneyland.
Timmy:	Well, my daddy is always at home, but he's always playing with his computer. It's his hobby.
Becky:	What's a hobby?
Timmy:	A hobby is something you do during your *seizure* time.
Becky:	(*Confused*) Oh.
Timmy:	Anyway, my daddy won't let me touch his computer. He says if I do, then I'll get sucked in and eaten by the giant spider that lives in the World Wide Web.
Becky:	You mean your daddy lives with you all the time?
Timmy:	Yeah. (*Pause*) Becky, does it make you sad that your daddy doesn't live at your house? 'Cause I can share my daddy with you.
Becky:	No, that's okay. See, I have a big sister, and she looks just like Barbie.
Timmy:	She has pointy plastic feet and everything?
Becky:	No.
Timmy:	She's only this tall? (*Holding up Barbie*)
Becky:	No.
Timmy:	She can turn her head all the way around, move her arms all the way around, and do the splits like this?! (*Does all three things with a Barbie doll*)
Becky:	Timmy! I said she looks just like Barbie. Anyway, when my daddy left, I used to cry lots and lots. But my big sister—who looks just like Barbie— told me not to cry. She said that I have a Heavenly Daddy who lives in my

heart—and he won't ever leave me or move away or stop loving me. Now when I am happy or sad or lonely or whatever, I can pray to Jesus. I close my eyes, and it feels like I walk right up to him and crawl on his lap, and he puts his arms around me and says, "Oh, Becky, I love you so much." So you see, I don't need your daddy.

Timmy: Who's Jesus?

Becky: Really?

Timmy: Yeah…who's Jesus?

Becky: He lived a long time ago, and even though he died once, he came back to life. So now he lives forever.

Timmy: Wow, that's cool! (*Pause*) Becky, is Jesus just for little girls whose daddies don't live with them anymore?

Becky: Oh no, Jesus is for everybody.

Timmy: Becky, I'm sorry I said my daddy loves me more than your daddy loves you. And I'm sorry I said you were the devil—because, really, you're just a big, hairy monster.

Becky: Timmy! (*Chases **Timmy** offstage*)

THE END.

"MOST LIKELY TO..."
BY EDDIE JAMES & TOMMY WOODARD WITH JEFF MAGUIRE & THE SKITIOTS

WHAT: Before you enter high school, what do you imagine it will be like? How does that concept change as the years go by? This sketch follows two friends as they go through high school, facing the challenges and changes each year brings. (Themes: friends, purpose)

WHO: Scott, Kelly

WHEN: Present day

WHY: John 15:13; Acts 20:24; Romans 10:1; 1 Corinthians 4:12

WEAR: (COSTUMES AND PROPS) Two backpacks (stuffed with pillows), two soft-drink cups, two day-planners, set of car keys, pen, a pair of sunglasses, something that creates a school bell sound

HOW: To demonstrate the beginning of each new year, make small changes in the appearance of each actor (e.g., a change of hair for Kelly, a change in Scott's style of walking). Whatever you choose, this will be a great challenge for your actors, who will be the best resource to make this skit look realistic.

SCENE ONE: FRESHMAN YEAR

*It's the very first day of high school. **Scott** and **Kelly** walk together, looking around in disbelief. They're wearing overstuffed backpacks cinched snugly around their shoulders, walking hunched over under the weight of their schoolbooks.*

Kelly: (*Amazed*) This place is huuuugggee!

Scott: I know; I can't believe it!

Kelly: What do they call this place again?

Scott:	I think they call it (*insert the name of your high school*).
Both:	(*In unison, drawn out in amazement*) High school.

Both face the audience and pan their eyes together across the stage, as if watching someone walk by—someone who is considerably taller and more massive than anyone they have ever seen before in their entire lives.

Scott:	Was that a senior? He had…(*motions to chin and under arm*) hair. Whoa.
Kelly:	(*Trying to pull it together*) Hey, do you know where room 12,462 is?
Scott:	Is that the A-wing or the B-wing?
Kelly:	I think it's the E-wing.
Scott:	There's an E-wing? This is all too much. My mind can't comprehend all the new changes! (*School bell is heard*) I think I'm hearing bells!
Kelly:	Whoa! I'm hearing them, too!
Both:	(*Pause and look at each other*) The tardy bell!
Kelly:	We're going to be tardy on our first day of high school! You know that goes on your permanent record!
Scott:	Run! Save yourself! Run!

*Both sprint together in a wild panic off the stage, as if being late to their first class would spell certain doom. While backstage, remove backpacks, put jacket on **Scott**, and change **Kelly's** hair to show that a year has passed.*

SCENE TWO: SOPHOMORE YEAR

Scott *and **Kelly** enter the stage together holding their soft-drink cups, carrying much lighter backpacks, and making blatant fun of the new freshmen. Their attitude is bitterly sarcastic and extremely know-it-all. **Scott** is swinging his mom's car keys in his hands.*

Kelly:	Hey freshman! Did Mommy pack your lunch? Huh? Yeah, I'm talking to you…

Scott:	Yeah, nice drink box, little fish. What? Are you about to cry? I better call a waaaammbullance!
Kelly:	What's that you're eating? Mmmm. Tuna Melt Surprise and a carton of two-week-old milk? (*Waving their cups in the air in a taunting way*) Too bad it's not an ice-cold Pepsi from Taco Bell.
Scott:	(*Waving his keys in the air above his head, shaking them occasionally as he talks*) Bet you wish you were sophomores like us!
Kelly:	Bet you wish you could sneak off campus like we just did!
Scott:	(*Suddenly notices vice principal walking by and stuffs his keys in his pocket frantically*) Hey, Mr. Lytle. Oh, this Taco Bell drink? Yeah, um...my mom brought this to me. She's the best mommy! See ya later, Mr. Lytle.
Kelly:	Did you just say "mommy"?
Scott:	Watch it. That was a close one. (*Pause*) Hey, Kelly, what are you doing this weekend?
Kelly:	I don't know. Why?
Scott:	Well, my friend invited me to some church deal. You want to come? (***Kelly*** *looks confused;* ***Scott*** *picks up on it*) Oh! Wait...no...it's not like we're gonna sit in the front row and be all like, "Thou shalt not." No, we sit in the back and make fun of the people who actually "shalt not." They always seem like a cult over there, and I thought it'd be fun to check it out. Want to? I'm drivin', 'cause (*major increase in volume, begins to vigorously flash keys to audience and imaginary freshmen*) I got my license. That's right, I'm driving. Who wants to come, 'cause I can drive! Gonna be traveling in style.
Kelly:	Got your mom's minivan, huh?
Scott:	Oh yeah! I just gotta take my little sister to ballet practice, but then the van's all mine! And did I mention? I'm drivin'!
Kelly:	Well, uh, thanks, Scott, but, um, Brad Smith invited me to his party this weekend, so I don't think I'll be able to make it.

Scott: Really? Brad Smith? The senior?

Kelly: Yeah. Well, actually, his sister's friend is friends with my friend, and she said one time that Brad smiled in my general direction. (*Short pause*) So, I'm invited.

Scott: Sounds like it to me. You're so lucky.

Both: (*Awkward pause*) Well, okay.

School bell rings.

Scott: (*Sarcastically*) Oh no, the tardy bell!

Kelly: (*Mocking the freshmen, watching as they run*) Look at the wittle freshmen wunning to cwass.

Scott: (*In Arnold Schwarzenegger voice*) Run little freshmen, before I squeeze you like a tube of toothpaste, and then three out of four dentists won't recommend you. Hope you make it.

Kelly: (*To **Scott***) Uh, the '80s called. They want that voice back.

Scott: (*Sheepishly*) I know…kind of stupid, wasn't it?

Both look around to see if anyone is watching—and then they, too, sprint off to class.

SCENE THREE: JUNIOR YEAR

Scott and Kelly walk together—day planners in hand and no backpacks—with totally exhausted looks on their faces. Scott yawns in weariness.

Kelly: (*Exasperated*) I have been living on a steady diet of NoDoz.

Scott: Tell me about it. (*Counting off his fingers*) I've got a 10-page research paper due tomorrow, three in-class essays, and I'm taking the SAT practice test four times on Thursday.

Kelly: Oh yeah? Well, I've got…

Scott: (*Cuts her off*) You know what, forget it. Don't even worry, 'cause (*as a ray of light begins to show, a break from the endless hours of study*) guess what's comin' up? (*Yelling with excitement*) Spring break!

*Both begin yelling and chanting. **Scott** pumps his arms as he circles the stage and does a little spring break dance. **Kelly** does the same.*

Kelly: (*Stops the dancing*) Scott, what are you doing for spring break?

Scott: You should come with me! I'm goin' to Mexico with…

Kelly: (*Extremely excited*) Mexico! I've always wanted to go! Party-party-part-y! I hear they sell you all kinds of mixed drinks, and they don't even check your ID in some places! How cool is that? Away from my parents, and a chance to hang out, check out the locals, and forget that these tests ever existed. (*Turns to see **Scott** looking a little stumped*) What is it, Scott?

Scott: Actually, Kell, I'm going down there with a group from the church I've been going to. It's supposed to be a real life-changing exp…

Kelly: Save it, Scott. (*Pause*) Oh my gosh—they've sucked you in, haven't they? So the rumors *are* true. You've joined the "Thou Shalt Not Club."

Scott: It's really not like that. The things I've been learning are pretty amazing, and I think it…

Kelly: Scott! Save it, I said! I'm not interested.

Scott: (*Pause*) What are they saying about me?

Kelly: What?

Scott: You said, "the rumors are true." So what are they saying about me?

Kelly: (*A little uncomfortable*) Well, they say you're getting a little religious—kind of turning into a Jesus Junior type, I guess.

Scott: It's so much more than just reli…

Kelly: Okay, Pastor Scott, I'm gone. I want to study a little more before the bell rings. (*Starts to walk away*)

Scott:	And the rumors about you…are they true?
Kelly:	(*Slight pause, keeps her back to **Scott**)* Yes. (*Her head is down a little, but not overly dramatic. **Kelly** then starts to walk offstage*)
Scott:	You…want to talk about it?

School bell rings.

Kelly:	Saved by the bell.
Scott:	I'm here for you if you need me, Kelly.

Kelly has already walked offstage. Scott heads for class.

SCENE FOUR: SENIOR YEAR

Kelly enters the stage alone. She walks to the center of the stage and places her hands over her face. Scott is wearing sunglasses. The mood is a little down. Kelly appears worn out and tired. Scott approaches her after a second or two. He looks a little unsure if the person he sees is his friend Kelly.

Scott:	Kelly? Hey, it's been months since we last talked. How have you been?
Kelly:	(*Sadly*) Okay. How about you?
Scott:	I'm going to class—(*he holds up a pen, showing it to the audience*)—totally pre-pared. Wow, this is it. We're seniors. Almost outta here. Pretty amazing, huh?
Kelly:	Yeah, I guess.
Scott:	Kelly, is there anything I can do for you?
Kelly:	(*Looking up at **Scott**, removing her hands from her face*) No. Not unless you can give me back these past four years I've wasted. Can you do that for me, Scott?
Scott:	(*A bit uncomfortable*) Uh, no…I can't, Kell.

Kelly:	(*In her own world, on the verge of tears*) I didn't think so…I'm so burned out. I guess my parents were right: There is no hope for me.
Scott:	(*Stands beside **Kelly***) Come on—that's not true. There's always hope.
Kelly:	(*Leans into **Scott's** shoulder*) Is this is where you try to invite me to church for the thousandth time and I turn you down again?
Scott:	Yes, and…I don't know. Is it?
Kelly:	(*Brief pause*) I don't know.
Scott:	I just want you to meet someone.
Kelly:	Yeah? I'm not that much to look at. You think this person will want to meet me?
Scott:	Definitely.

Kelly leans into Scott's shoulder as ***Scott*** hugs her and holds her. *They exit.*

THE END.

"FRIENDS TELL FRIENDS EVERYTHING"

**BY EDDIE JAMES & TOMMY WOODARD WITH
DREW FLETCHER & ROB CAROTHERS**

WHAT: Two friends agree to tell each other absolutely everything, no matter how embarrassing. They share just about everything with each other, except the one thing that matters most. (Themes: evangelism, friends, trust, remorse, life experience)

WHO: David, Steve

WHEN: Various moments over 13 years

WHY: Ephesians 1:18-19; 1 Peter 4:11; Revelation 2:3-5

WEAR:
(COSTUMES
AND PROPS)
To make each year stand out, use baseball caps for the little kids, glasses for middle school students, and graduation robes for the high school scene. For the dance scene, play "My Heart Will Go On" by Celine Dion (from the *Titanic* soundtrack) or another popular love song.

HOW: The story is told in three vignettes. The characters age throughout the story, which should be denoted through voices, mannerisms, and costuming.

---

*The skit starts with **David**, always playing the character much older than the other three parts, talking to the audience.*

David: (*To audience*) I remember the first time I met Steve—we couldn't have been more than five years old. I had no idea we would grow up together. We became best friends. We shared everything, always under the same philosophy: *Friends tell friends everything.* We had no secrets.

***Steve**, age five, enters, rubbing his rear. Need quick pace to this dialogue.*

David (age *five*):   Hi, whatchya doin'?

Steve: Nothin'.

David:	How come yer rubbin' yer rear?
Steve:	'Cuz.
David:	'Cuz why?
Steve:	Got in trouble.
David:	You got in trouble?
Steve:	Yeah. Got a spankin' and a time out.
David:	Got a spankin' *and* a time out? Why? What were ya doin'?
Steve:	'Sperimentin'.
David:	'Sperimentin'?
Steve:	Yeah.
David:	What were ya 'sperimentin' with?
Steve:	Parakeet.
David:	Parakeet?
Steve:	Yeah.
David:	(*Laughs*) Whadja do with the parakeet?
Steve:	Put him on my Big Wheel.
David:	You put him on yer Big Wheel?
Steve:	Yeah.
David:	(*Laughs*) Whadja use to get him on the Big Wheel?
Steve:	Duct tape.
David:	Duct tape?

Steve:	Yeah.
David:	(*Laughs*) You used duct tape to put yer parakeet on yer Big Wheel?
Steve:	Yeah.
David:	How come?
Steve:	Wanted to see what kind of noise it would make.
David:	What kind of noise *did* it make?
Steve:	Kind of a tweet, clunk, tweet, clunk, tweet, crack.
David:	Cool.
Steve:	Yeah.
David:	How is the parakeet now?
Steve:	He was doing okay 'til we tried to take the duct tape off.
David:	So ya got a spankin' and a time out?
Steve:	Yeah.
David:	If you're supposed to be in time out, how come yer out here with me?
Steve:	Can't tell ya.
David:	How come?
Steve:	'Cuz.
David:	Come on, friends tell friends everything.
Steve:	We're friends?
David:	Yeah, I guess...Don't make a big deal out of it.
Steve:	'Kay.

David: So how come yer out here with me?

Steve: Yer my punishment.

David: I'm yer punishment?

Steve: Yeah, my dad said I had to go play with the new kid.

David: Oh.

Steve: (*Pause*) So.

David: (*Pause*) So.

Steve: So whatchya wanna do?

David: I dunno, whadda *you* wanna do?

Steve: I dunno, whadda *you* wanna do?

David: I dunno, whadda *you* wanna do?

Steve: Got a parakeet?

David: No.

Steve: Loser.

David: (*Eager to please*) Got a cat.

Steve: Cool. Got any duct tape?

David: No.

Steve: Loser.

David: Got a staple gun!

Steve: Cool. Here kitty, kitty.

Steve exits.

David: (*Older, to audience*) That's how it started. We were inseparable. We did everything together, went everywhere together, and told each other everything—because friends tell friends everything. We were together even through the "awkward" years.

Steve, age 12, enters. *Steve* and *David* are now in sixth grade. *Utilize glasses, retainers, or high voices to show they're awkward and just hitting puberty.*

Steve: Hey, Davey.

David: (*Voice cracks constantly*) I told you, my name is *Da-vid.*

Steve: What's wrong with yer voice?

David: My mom says I'm becoming a man.

Steve: Cool. So, you coming to the Jedi Club meeting tonight?

David: Can't.

Steve: Whaddya mean "can't"? You gotta come to the Jedi Club meeting!

David: Nope, can't.

Steve: How come?

David: Can't tell you.

Steve: Can't tell me? Why?

David: Just can't.

Steve: Come on, friends tell friends everything.

David: All right. I can't go to the Jedi Club meeting 'cuz I'm goin' to the "Spring Fling" dance.

Steve: Yer goin' to the dance?

David: Yep.

Steve:	Who ya goin' to the dance with?
David:	Jenny.
Steve:	Yer goin' to the dance with a girl?
David:	Yep.
Steve:	But what about the Jedi Club? You can't miss this meeting.
David:	How come? What's so special about this meeting?
Steve:	Can't tell you.
David:	Can't tell me?
Steve:	Nope.
David:	Come on, friends tell friends everything.
Steve:	Okay, fine. Yer getting a promotion.
David:	A promotion?
Steve:	Yep, from Obi-Wan Kenobi, to Obi-*Two* Kenobi!
David:	Wow, I gotta be there for that.
Steve:	What about the dance with Jenny?
David:	I won't go.
Steve:	What? Are you crazy? Jenny is like the most popular girl in school—you gotta go to the dance with her! Do it for all us geeks who will be at the Jedi Club tonight!
David:	Nope, don't want to.
Steve:	Don't want to? How come?
David:	Can't tell you.

Steve:	How come?
David:	Just can't.
Steve:	Come on, friends tell friends everything. Why don't you want to go to the dance?
David:	I can't dance.
Steve:	You can't dance?
David:	Nope, I can't bust a move, raise the roof, or get jiggy with it. I don't even know who let the dogs out!
Steve:	(*Realizes this calls for drastic measures*) Oh brother. All right, close the door.
David:	What?
Steve:	Close the door.
David:	Why?
Steve:	Just do it; I'm gonna help you. But don't tell anyone about this! Shut the door.
David:	You're scaring me.
Steve:	Just let me turn on my CD player.
David:	(Titanic *soundtrack is heard playing*) You've got the soundtrack from *Titanic*?
Steve:	It's my mom's!
David:	Suuuuure it is.
Steve:	Just come over here.
David:	Now what?
Steve:	Put yer arms around me.

David: What?

Steve: Just do it!

David complies. He puts his hands on *Steve's* waist a little too hard.

Steve: Hey, yer not moving furniture here, buddy. Hold me like I'm Jenny.

David: I can't picture you as Jenny.

Steve: (*Pretends to be Jenny*) Ooooooh, I'm so excited to be dancing with this big strong Jedi warrior. He is the coolest Jedi in the galaxy. (*Normal voice*) Now sway back and forth a little.

David: 'Kay.

Steve: How does that feel?

David: Uncomfortably comfortable.

Steve: Now yer getting it.

They both begin to move to the music, then suddenly realize they're dancing together, scream, and jump away from each other. ***Steve*** *exits.*

David: Steve was always there for me all the way through high school. All the time we were growing up together, I was going to church, and I knew Steve wasn't. He knew I went, but we never talked about it. I never shared my faith with him. As we got closer to graduating from high school and enrolled in different colleges, I knew our lives would take us away from each other. I knew I needed to tell Steve about Jesus. So I asked him to come over on graduation day.

Steve, age 18, enters.

Steve: Hey, buddy, ready to go?

David: Almost. Come on in and sit down.

Steve: Okay, but we don't have much time.

David:	I know, but I need to talk to you.
Steve:	What's up?
David:	Well, after graduation, we're gonna be going our separate ways.
Steve:	You're not going to Jenny's party?
David:	Of course I'm going to Jenny's party, you idiot. Stop fooling around; this is serious!
Steve:	Okay, but hurry up, we're late.
David:	Look, you're going to run into all kinds of new situations in college and life after college, and, well…
Steve:	What?
David:	Well, you need to be careful out there.
Steve:	Be careful out there? That's what you wanted to tell me? Be careful out there?
David:	Well…
Steve:	What is it?
David:	It's just hard to…
Steve:	Hard to what? Come on, friends tell friends everything.

They pause and smile at each other.

David:	(*Deep breath*) Okay.
Steve:	Look, I can tell this is important, but we're really late, so why don't you tell me in the car?
David:	Okay.
Steve:	I'll go start the car; you grab your cap and gown and come out.

David:	Okay.
Steve:	But you'll tell me in the car, right?
David:	Yes.
Steve:	You promise you'll tell me in the car?
David:	Yes, I'll tell you.

Steve walks upstage and stands facing *David. David* turns to the audience.

David:	(*Older*) I never told him. Why? Why was it so hard to tell him about Jesus? We shared everything because friends tell friends everything. I told him about every movie I ever saw and every date I ever went on; but when it came time to share my faith, I never told him. (*Pause*) Yesterday morning an 18-wheeler collided with three cars. Seven people were injured, and two were killed. One was Steve. (*Steve pauses and turns to exit, then stops and turns around*) I don't know if he ever came to know Christ. What I do know is that I missed out on the opportunity to tell my best friend about the most important thing in life. It'd been years since I'd seen or heard from Steve, but he played a role in my life daily. You see, I've decided not to make that mistake with anyone again. If friends tell friends everything, then it all begins with telling them the main thing. (*They exit*)

THE END.

"THIS YEAR WILL BE DIFFERENT"
BY EDDIE JAMES & TOMMY WOODARD

WHAT: In this skit, two characters look forward to a new year and make a list of resolutions to change things in their lives. (Themes: change, dedication, seeking, trust)

WHO: Character 1, Character 2

WHEN: Present day

WHY: Proverbs 3:5-6; Mark 12:30; 2 Corinthians 8:11

WEAR: Everyday, casual attire
(COSTUMES AND PROPS)

HOW: Memorization is crucial to this skit. Make sure the two actors go back and forth so there aren't any long pauses between lines. The actors never look at one another as they tell the story. With a couple of minor changes, this could be done either by guys or by girls.

Both: This year will be different...

Character 2: This year I'll eat less.

Character 1: This year I'll eat more. I'm really wanting to...

Character 2: ...figure out more about what I believe. I'm going to spend time...

Character 1: ...making my body a living monument for the ladies. (*Does some flexing*) I just need to...

Character 2: ...learn to wait. I'm always wanting things instantly. I need patience—now! This year I'll...

Character 1:   ...be nicer to my parents. (*Yelling offstage*) What, Mom? Hold on! I said, hold on! Mooommm! The trash will go out in a minute!! (*To audience*) I wish she'd...

Character 2:   ...notice me. This year I'm going to walk right up to Casey, the girl who's had my heart since seventh grade, and tell her how I...

Character 1:   ...need peace in my life. I'm so nervous all the time. I have this little twitch. (*Shows audience*) Maybe it's from all of those lattes, mochas, and frappuccinos. That stuff can't be good for me. I just can't seem to get...

Character 2:   ...my pits to stop sweating. (*Holds arms up to show wet spots*) How does this keep happening? I know: I'll shower more, I'll scrub more, I'll...

Both: ...be better than I've ever been before in my life!

Character 1:   If I'm going to make this year count, I need to do some things differently. I can't keep going at the pace I'm going. Help me, God!

Character 2:   God? (*Looking up as if talking to God*) Did you forget about me? Are you even up there? Don't get me wrong—I want to believe in you; I guess I just need...

Character 1:   ...the strength to change. (*Looking up as if talking to God*) Honestly, though, I don't know if I really want to. I'm comfortable. I've believed in you since I was a little kid. I have fun; I don't do anything too risky. I have a good life. I know you want the best for me. So why don't *I* want the best for me? I guess I'm...

Character 2:   ...afraid the Bible will have some things in it that I may not understand or that I wouldn't want to give my whole life over to. The thing is, I don't know where to...

Both: ...start.

Character 1:   Starting tomorrow, I'm living my life differently. God's way—not so much the world's way. It's wrong not to use my time better and my talents for God. I can't continue to stay quiet about the great things God has done in my life. That was never meant to be...

Character 2:   …a secret. (*To audience*) Can I tell you a secret? I feel separated from… something. Sounds weird, doesn't it? I feel like I need something, but what I need is bigger than anything this world could ever offer. It's like I'm waiting for someone to walk up to me and say…

Character 1:   (*To God*)…here it is. Take it. I want my life to be something much more than what I see. Take this little bit of faith that I have, God.

Character 2:   Take this doubting soul, God. Help me find what I'm looking for. Give me hope.

Both: I just can't wait another year.

THE END.

"PIECE OF A PEACE"

BY EDDIE JAMES & TOMMY WOODARD WITH JOHNNY BAKER

WHAT: As this skit illustrates, everybody longs for peace in his life. As each character searches for peace, they learn there's really only one way to find it. (Themes: peace, hope)

WHO: Barry, Larry, Teri, Jerry

WHEN: Present day

WHY: Psalm 4:8, 29:11; John 8:12; Philippians 4:7

WEAR: Three chairs, duffel bag, battery-powered flashlight
(COSTUMES
AND PROPS)

HOW: Play this skit with a lot of energy and maintain a good rhythm. Think of these characters as Jerry, Elaine, George, and Kramer from *Seinfeld* to give the performance its comedic edge.

Barry enters carrying a duffel bag. (Note: Fill duffel bag with clothes and pack around a flashlight so that when the bag is opened, the light will shine on his face.) *Larry* enters and sits next to *Barry.* They may know each other, but not well.

Larry: (*i.e., George Costanza*) Hey, what's up?

Barry: (*i.e., Jerry Seinfeld*) Not much. You?

Larry: Nothin'. Hey, what's in the bag?

Barry: The bag?

Larry: Yeah, the bag.

Barry: Peace.

Larry: A piece of what?

Barry: Not "piece," peace. (*He holds up fingers in a peace sign. This should be done every time the word "peace" is said*)

Larry: Peace! You got peace in that bag?

Barry: Oh yeah. It's great.

Larry: Well, could I see peace?

Barry: Uh, sure, yeah.

Barry opens bag. Light shines on their faces.

Larry: Whoa, could I have a piece of that peace?

Barry: No, you can't have a piece of my peace. It's *my* peace.

Larry: Okay, well, how about a chunk of that peace?

Barry: A chunk of peace is the same thing as a piece of peace.

Teri (i.e., Elaine) enters and sits on the other side of Barry.

Teri: Hey guys, what's up?

Larry: Not much...Hey, guess what?

Teri: What?

Larry: Barry has peace in the bag.

Teri: Really? Could I see?

Barry: Sure.

Barry opens bag. Again light shines on their faces.

Larry: He said I couldn't have a piece or even a chunk of that peace.

Teri: What about a slice of the peace?

Barry: No. Asking for a slice is just like asking for a chunk, which is just like asking for a piece. I'm not giving you any.

Jerry (i.e., Kramer) enters.

Jerry: Hi guys. Teri. What's going on?

Teri: We're just talking about what Barry has in his bag.

Jerry: What's he got?

Larry: Peace.

Jerry: A piece? A piece? Man, stay away. I don't want any trouble! (*He starts to get hysterical*) Put the bag down! Put the bag down, man. I was just on my way to visit my old Aunt Edna…

Teri: With the mustache?

Jerry and Teri both make disgusted faces.

Barry: You've got it all backward. The peace I have won't harm or hurt you.

Jerry: (*Stops crying suddenly*) It won't?

Larry: Apparently, it's not that kind of piece.

Barry: It's not that kind of piece. (*Opens bag*)

Jerry: Gimme. I want. I want. I need it. I need that peace. Gimme a piece of that peace.

Larry: Just a chunk.

Teri: A slice. Gimme a slice!

Barry: Would you look at yourselves? You can't have a piece, chunk, slice, morsel, tidbit…

Jerry:	A smidgeon?
Barry:	Not even a smidgeon of my peace. It's my peace. It was given to me.
Larry:	*Given* to you?
Jerry:	By whom?
Barry:	I know a guy.
Teri:	You have a guy?
Larry:	You have a peace guy?
Barry:	You could call him a friend for life.
Teri:	What do we have to do to get this peace?
Barry:	Nothing.
All:	Nothing?
Larry:	Then give us some of that peace! You're hoarding the peace, Barry. You are a peace hoarder.
Barry:	Why should you be happy with only a chunk, slice, or smidgeon of peace? You can get your own. After all, real peace is free.
Teri:	I want real peace.
Jerry:	Oh yeah. I'm in.
Larry:	Why don't you take us to your peace guy?
Barry:	Right this way.

They all start to exit. As they are going off…

Larry:	(*Pointing to the bag*) Can I hold the peace?
Barry:	No.

Larry:	Please?
Barry:	No.
Larry:	Please?
Barry:	No.
Larry:	You're still hoarding the peace, Barry.
Barry:	No, Larry. It's called keeping the peace. (*They exit*)

THE END.

"SAM GOODY & THE CASE OF THE SELFLESS FATHER"

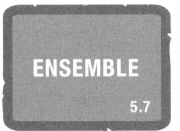

ENSEMBLE

5.7

BY EDDIE JAMES & TOMMY WOODARD WITH JOHNNY BAKER & MARK WALLACE

WHAT: Here is a comedy noir involving a down-on-his-luck P.I. and a beautiful dame trying to solve the mystery of her father's death. (Themes: fathers, searching, salvation, love)

WHO: Narrator, Goody, Actor, Susie

WHEN: 1940s

WHY: Matthew 7:7; 2 Corinthians 5:21; Philippians 2:5-11

WEAR:
(COSTUMES AND PROPS)
Costumes will really help with the feel of this skit. Watch old detective movies and use your imagination. Additional props: business card, newspaper, photograph, eye chart, breath mints, pen, pad of paper, jigsaw puzzle, desk, pizza box, Chinese food, Pepto-Bismol®, can of beans, paper bag

HOW: This script is structured for three actors, but for variety's sake, the "Actor" parts can be played by different individuals. Also, since the script requires a gun, please feel free to pantomime the gun if it goes against your group's sensibilities to use a toy gun onstage. Then put your tongue in your cheek and have fun.

---

*Onstage paces **Sam Goody,** an old-school private eye. The first thing we hear is the offstage* **Narrator.**

Narrator: It's 1946, a cold night in midtown Manhattan. I'm detective Sam Goody. I come from a long line of music lovers. I was in my office late that night. I work late every night. I was trying to track down a one-armed man. But I couldn't. I had no leads. I had nowhere to go. I'd spent an arm and a leg trying to track down this guy. I guess that puts him a step ahead of me. Where are you, one-armed man? I looked out my window. Outside it was cold, damp, murky, meeky, and stinky. I thought to myself:

Goody: *I'd rather be skiing.*

Narrator: I took a whiff of the air. (*Goody smells the air and starts to cough*) The air can tell you a lotta things. Tonight it was telling me one thing: Bad news was right around the corner.

Actor: (*Enters as paperboy carrying a newspaper*) Bad news! Get your bad news here!

Goody: (*Grabs a paper and reads front page*) Just as I thought: bad news, right around the corner.

Narrator: And then she walked in. The prettiest dame I ever did see.

Susie enters.

Goody: That's the prettiest dame I ever did see.

Narrator: As I started to walk toward her, I knew she was trouble.

Goody: (*Takes her hand and kisses it*) What's your name, Doll Face?

Susie: Susie H. Trouble.

Goody: I don't buy it. (*Susie reaches in her purse and pulls out a business card*) Amazing. It *is* Trouble. What seems to be the trouble, Trouble?

Susie: Well, I seem to be in a little bit of trouble.

Goody: What sort of trouble?

Susie: Serious trouble.

Goody: Double trouble?

Susie: No, single trouble.

Goody: Oh. Well then, I'm not too worried.

Susie: I'm looking for the truth.

Goody: Okay, I'm wearing Superman underwear.

Susie:	No, not that truth. I'm looking for the truth about my father. He died in a freak circus accident 15 years ago.
Goody:	You're joking.
Susie:	No, if I were joking, I'd say, "A horse walked into a bar and the bartender asked him, 'Why the long face?'"
Goody:	Mylanta, you're serious. So what can I do for you?
Susie:	Well, like I said, my father died in a freak circus accident 15 years ago, and I'm trying to find the truth about it.
Goody:	So, that's where I come in, huh? Stick my neck out on the line. Walk out there into the cruel world for the sake of a beautiful dame. Well, I'll tell ya…Mylanta, I'll do it.
Susie:	(*Digs in purse and pulls out photo*) I have a picture of him in here somewhere. Ah, here it is.
Goody:	(*Looks at photo*) Kind of a heavy guy with a large nose, wouldn't you say?
Susie:	No, he's the man on *top* of the elephant.
Goody:	Right. I'm a private investigator—P. I. I was just testing your eyes, Ms. Trouble.
Susie:	I don't mind being tested, Mr. Goody.
Goody:	All right, read that chart over there.

Actor *enters with eye chart.*

Susie:	(*Covers one eye*) C-T-O-M-B-X.
Goody:	Other eye.
Susie:	A-D-L-N-Y-Z.
Goody:	Twenty-twenty. All right. Well, try this on for size: What is the current average rainfall in the Amazon basin?

Susie:	Forty-seven point eight nine six inches per year.
Goody:	Mylanta, you're good. What's your story?
Susie:	My father died in a freak circus accident 15 years ago.
Goody:	Déjà vu. I swear I've heard that story somewhere before.
Susie:	I've already told it to you, Mr. Goody.
Goody:	That's right.
Susie:	Now, there is one more clue.
Narrator:	As she leaned in to tell me the clue, I could only think of one thing.
Goody:	(*Pulls out a container of mints*) Breath mint?

Susie, offended, starts to leave.

Narrator:	And with that, Doll Face started to walk out of my life. I had to do something quick, so I yelled to her.
Goody:	Susie, wait! I'm only saying this because I care. You know, there are a lot of decaffeinated brands that are just as tasty as regular coffee.
Susie:	(*Perplexed*) Uh…goodbye, Mr. Goody.
Narrator:	And with that, Doll Face was gone. But she did give me some information to help solve the case. First of all, her father, Jack Ringling, was a big circus tycoon. Second, she admitted that she'd married into Trouble—and I mean a whole *family* of Troubles. Her husband, a man named Imen, was a good man, but things didn't work out for Mr. and Mrs. Trouble. They were later divorced, although she kept his last name. To this day, I don't know why she did that.
	Finally, there was the clue Susie gave me: the clue to help solve the case. She said her husband only had *one arm*. Hmmm, now his name makes sense to me. There it goes again, that one-armed man thing. He pops up in everything I do. So I wondered, *How does a detective find a one-armed man?* I did the first thing that came to my mind.

Goody: (*Calls out*) One-armed man! Looking for a one-armed man! Anyone? Going once, twice, come on!

Narrator: Yelling out that window was unproductive. So I decided to do something else—Plan B. I went to the *Manhattan Gazette*. I took out a want ad. (**Goody** *writes on paper*) "Lonely P.I. seeks soul mate." Wait no, that's for later.

Goody: (*Looks to audience*) Hey, it gets lonely at the top. And I should know; I live on the fifty-fourth floor.

Narrator: I tried again. (**Goody** *writes at his desk*) "Looking for all one-armed men who love the circus." (*Thinks*) Now why would a one-armed man come here? Why would a one-armed man walk through my door? (**Goody** *writes again*) Oh, yes. "Free doughnuts." After that the rest of my day was pointless. No one-armed men came to my door at all. I knew I had to do something quick. Then it happened, late that evening, when what should I explore, but someone tapping, tapping on my chamber door. Nevermore, nevermore. When someone knocks on a P.I.'s door, it can be dangerous. So I did what every P.I. would do: I took out my piece. (**Goody** *pulls out a puzzle piece and puts in into the puzzle that is nearly complete on his desk*)

Goody: I've been looking for that. (*Grabs a gun from his desk*)

Narrator: So I started to inch toward the door. Slowly, carefully, not knowing who could be there, I tiptoed, I danced, I leaped…

*Have fun with this; the **Narrator** may want to just surprise the actor playing **Goody** and give different stage directions that **Goody** must act out as he approaches and opens the door.*

Actor: (*As pizza guy*) Pizza!

Goody: I didn't order any pizza.

Actor: Free gift from Ms. Trouble. (*Exits*)

Narrator: Trouble was sending me pizza. That could only mean one thing…(*pause*) free pizza! Then came another knock on my door. (**Goody** *opens door*)

Actor:	(*As Chinese food delivery guy*) Mu Shu Pork and egg rolls, compliments of Ms. Trouble.
Narrator:	Chinese food and pizza—I could only think of two words…(*Brief pause*) Pepto-Bismol. Then came yet another knock on the door.
Actor:	(*As Pepto delivery guy*) Pepto-Bismol, compliments of Ms. Trouble.
Goody:	Mylanta, she's good.
Narrator:	As I looked over my food, I did something a P.I. should never do. That's right; I left my door open. When you leave the door open, you never know what kind of Tom, Dick, or Harry will walk through.
Actor:	Hello? Hello?
Goody:	(*Pointing gun at **Actor***) What's your name?
Actor:	Tom Dick Harry.
Goody:	You're kidding.
Actor:	No.
Goody:	Come on, spill the beans. (***Actor** picks up can of beans*) Not on the floor—I just mopped! Let the cat out of the bag. (***Actor** picks up bag as if to dump a cat out of it*) Not here, I'm allergic to those things. You know what I'm talking about. I want answers. Start singing like a canary! (***Actor** begins to whistle like a bird, maybe even flapping his arms*) Stop taking me literally. The jig is up! What do you want?
Actor:	I have some information that will help you find your truth.
Goody:	What do you know about the truth, huh? What do you know about Susie H. Trouble and her father who died in a freak circus accident 15 years ago, huh? What do you know about it?
Actor:	I'm only the plumber. Are you talking about Mr. Ringling?
Goody:	Maybe I am and maybe I'm not.

Actor:	Come closer, I've got a story to tell you. Little closer. Little closer. (*Actor and **Goody** stand nose to nose*) Ah, too close. (***Goody** takes a step back*) One night Mr. Ringling was at his circus, and his daughter was about to be stepped on by an elephant—but he jumped out of nowhere and saved her life.
Goody:	That's a gruesome story. How am I supposed to tell a beautiful dame like her that her father got stepped on by an elephant in order to save her life?
Actor:	As gruesome as that may sound, he laid down his own life so she could live. Remember to tell her about the life she has now—and regardless of anything in her past, she can live life, and live it abundantly.
Goody:	Yeah, right.
Actor:	Sink?
Goody:	What?
Actor:	Sink. Where's the sink? I need to unclog it before I have to go to my other job.
Goody:	You must be thinking of the community sink down on the fifty-third floor.
Actor:	Oh, thank you. (*Exits*)
Narrator:	Before I could blink an eye, Doll Face walked in again.
Susie:	So what'd you find out, Detective?
Goody:	Bad news: It doesn't look like the Yankees are going to win the pennant this year.
Susie:	My father, Mr. Goody.
Goody:	Oh, yes, your father. He died in a freak circus accident 15 years ago.
Susie:	Tell me something I don't know.
Goody:	I sleep with a teddy bear.

Susie: Mr. Goody! My father?

Narrator: Her father. She wanted the truth, the whole truth, and nothing but the truth, so help me God. I turned around, and then it hit me: Mylanta, she's beautiful. That was of no consequence right now. Right now she needed words from me. Words from me that would heal her soul.

Goody: You know I think I know what your father would say if he were still alive today. He'd tell you he loves you. He always did love you. He loved you so much he even laid down his life for you.

Susie: Really? (*Tearing up*) I needed to hear that. Thank you, Mr. Goody. It feels good to be loved by a father.

Goody: Oh, and one more thing: If you ever want a man to love you, treat you like a lady, start a family, and grow old with you—I think you know where to look.

Susie: I do, thank you. Tom Dick Harry is such a wonderful fellow, and he taught me how to make a Slurpee. Goodbye.

Goody returns to his desk, sits down, and picks up the newspaper. Lights fade.

Narrator: And with that, the case of Mr. Ringling was closed—but there were many things still running through my mind. I kept thinking about the one-armed man. What did the one-armed man mean to my life? Now I knew who he was. He was Trouble. But how could I ever find him? I tell you, in that moment, in my office, I felt like a fugitive. And then there was Susie H. Trouble. Well, she ended up marrying Tom Dick Harry. And by the way, Tom Dick Harry's last name was Barnum, and his best friend's name was Bailey. So the legend Mr. Ringling began with his circus continues—if you catch my drift.

Well, that's my job. Seven days a week I work in this P.I. office. To some people, I'm a hero; to others, I'm just a lonely P.I. still searching for a soul mate—and a one-armed man named Imen Trouble. I used to say that trouble would always find me, but now...I guess you could say I'm the one who's looking for trouble.

THE END.

"WHO'S SERVING WHOM?"
BY EDDIE JAMES & TOMMY WOODARD WITH THE SKITIOTS

WHAT:	Through a series of vignettes, the true meaning of the word "service" is stretched, hidden, and finally uncovered. (Themes: servanthood, humility, compassion)
WHO:	Bobby, Karen, Shelter Worker, John, Kyle, Mrs. Evans, Peter, James, John
WHEN:	Present day; biblical times
WHY:	Matthew 20:28; 2 Corinthians 9:12; Hebrews 12:28
WEAR: (COSTUMES AND PROPS)	Modern-day clothes
HOW:	Refer to ensemble notes in chapter introduction.

---

*SCENE ONE: Begins with **Bobby** and **Karen** behind the counter at a soup kitchen. Both should be dressed in a manner completely inappropriate for serving food.*

Bobby: Man, serving in a real soup kitchen is so awesome! It's like something you'd see in the movies!

Karen: I know. This is what good people do. We're officially "good people"!

Bobby: I know. We get to work with real, live, homeless people! (*To homeless person*) Hey, homie!

Karen: (*To homeless person*) And that's an awesome jacket! (*To **Bobby***) Praise God for people like us.

Shelter Worker: Hey, guys, it's almost closing time, so thank you so much for coming out. I really appreciate all your hard work today.

Bobby: It was our pleasure.

Karen: Well…that's what good people do!

Bobby: And you know what? We figured out that if you pour water in the mashed potatoes, they stop coming back for seconds!

Shelter Worker: Uhh, that's not necessary, but thanks for trying to help.

Bobby: Just trying to save you some money.

Shelter Worker: Well, thanks for your thoughtfulness. So are you interested in coming back and doing this again?

Both: Oh yeah, for sure!

Shelter Worker: What are you two doing next weekend?

Both: Beyoncé in concert!!

Bobby: Beyoncé, man! She's in town.

Karen: Hey, you should come with us!

Bobby: Yeah, we have an extra ticket 'cause Dale's not coming.

Shelter Worker: I can't, I'm going to be doing this again next weekend. Actually, I do this three times a week.

Karen: Three times?

Bobby: How often do these people have to eat?

Karen: Yeah, beggars can't be choosers!

Shelter Worker: I just feel like it's more valuable to spend my time here than anywhere else.

(*Dramatic pause*)

Karen: You know what? You're right. This was great.

Bobby: Yeah, and Beyoncé will be back in town another time.

Shelter Worker: All right, I'll sign you guys up for next Saturday then. (*Begins to walk away*)

(*Pause…**Karen** and **Bobby** look at each other and then burst into laughter*)

Karen: Oh my goodness! (*Looking at **Bobby***) I thought you were serious for a minute.

Bobby: You were kidding, right?

Karen: Of course. Come on—give up a night out for these down-and-outs? I don't think so. And you! (*Looking at **Shelter Worker***) You should be in the movies.

Bobby: She's right; you are really good! You totally had us going with that whole "three times a week" thing.

Shelter Worker: I was serious.

(***Karen** and **Bobby** stop laughing*)

Bobby: Well…I guess you're just a better person than we are. Let's go, Karen.

Karen: (*Whispers back*) Yeah, I'm never coming back! (*To **Shelter Worker***) Can't wait 'til next weekend!

Bobby: (*Whispers to **Karen***) You wouldn't miss the Beyoncé concert, right?

Karen: (*Whispers back*) No way! (*To **Shelter Worker**, waving*) See you Saturday!

Bobby: (*To **Karen***) That guy was a huge dork!

Karen: (*To **Bobby***) Yeah, great guy. (*To **Shelter Worker***) You're a loser!

***Bobby** and **Karen** look at each other, realizing her mistake, and exit.*

SCENE TWO: **Kyle** *is standing on* **Mrs. Evans'** *lawn after mowing it. He has a pair of hedge trimmers in his hands.* **John,** *whose job it is, hurries onto the stage as if running late.*

John:	Oh man, what am I going to do? (*Reaches* **Kyle**) Wow! How did you do all this?
Kyle:	Well, John, I knew you were out late last night and you probably wouldn't finish Mrs. Evans' yard, so I decided to come over and just do it for you.
John:	This is unbelievable! I can't believe you would do this. I mean, you even trimmed the bushes into little animals! There's an elephant, there's a flamingo, and there's a giraffe!
Kyle:	It's actually a llama. I learned how to do it this morning on the Internet.
John:	Well, it looks great. What do I owe you?
Kyle:	Nothing, I just wanted to be a helper today. You know what, let's make this a special treat for Mrs. Evans. Don't make her pay today. Tell her that...

Mrs. Evans *enters, gazing at the lawn.*

John:	Oh...hi, Mrs. Evans!
Mrs. Evans:	Oh my! John, I just came out here to see how far along you were with the yard, and it looks incredible!
John:	(*Hesitantly*) Uh, thank you, but...
Mrs. Evans:	I decided to come out here and give you your check right now!
John:	Oh, great. Actually, you know what, I can't take all the credit for this.
Mrs. Evans:	What do you mean?
John:	I didn't do this alone. I can't take all the credit for myself. I needed help...I needed help from a close friend of mine. A little friend I like to call...Perseverance! I wouldn't have been able to get up this early and get through all the heat without him.

Mrs. Evans:	Oh, I know what you mean. This is wonderful, John. I mean, you even trimmed the bushes into little animals! Let's see—there's an elephant, a flamingo, and oh, look, even a giraffe!
Kyle:	It's a llama.
John:	I'm sorry, Kyle thinks it's a llama, but you're actually right. It is obviously a giraffe. Yeah, I learned how to do that on the Internet this morning. (*Looks at **Kyle***) You know what, Mrs. Evans, that's not it. I still have to thank one more person. It's because of this person's thoughtfulness that I got this yard finished. Without him, none of this would be done. And it's thanks to my good friend…John Deere and his trusty lawn mowers! They're incredible!
Mrs. Evans:	Well, I don't know about John's deer, but thank you so much for making an old woman's day. John, I think you're the one who's incredible. (***Mrs. Evans*** *exits*)
John:	Thank you. (*Long pause…turns to say something to **Kyle***)
Kyle:	Yeah, she's right, John…you're incredible. (*Exits*)

Freeze and fade out, or characters exit.

SCENE THREE: Three of Jesus' disciples sit on the floor, prepare for a meal, and are arguing among themselves.

Peter:	Man, I'm starved. James, do you know what we're eating tonight?
James:	I'm not sure, Peter. I hope there's something besides juice and crackers. I need some protein!
John:	Come on, James, it's a Passover meal. You know what we get to eat.
James:	Oh yeah. Man, I forgot.
Peter:	John, you're always on top of things! How do you do it?
John:	Simple…I'm the greatest disciple ever.

Peter:	I don't think so. *I'm* the greatest...I mean, come on...I was the one who walked on water, wasn't I?
James:	Yeah, but you also managed to fall in it! That disqualifies you and, in turn, makes *me* the greatest!
John:	Wait, wait—I'm getting a revelation! Yes—I've got it. My revelation is: Both of you are nuts! You (*to **Peter***) are dumb as rock. And you (*to **James***) ...you...you haven't really done anything. Not to mention both of you have the stinkiest feet I have ever smelled! I'm clearly the greatest of all the disciples!
Peter:	(*To **Jesus***) Hey, Jesus, out of everyone in this room, who is the greatest? (***Peter** visually "locks on" to what **Jesus** is doing and just starts staring at him*)
John:	Yeah, Jesus, tell them I'm the greatest so we can stop arguing and start eating. (***John** also stops talking and begins staring at **Jesus***)
James:	(*Oblivious to what is going on*) Forget it, you guys, he's not listening. I don't care what you think—I know I'm the greatest.

Peter and *John* look at *James* and shush him.

James:	What's he doing?
John:	He's washing Bartholomew's feet!
James:	Wait a minute—it looks like he's going to wash all our feet.
Peter:	No way...there is no way I'm going to let Jesus wash my feet.
James:	It doesn't make sense. He's the greatest person I've ever known, yet he's on his knees acting like a servant.
John:	The greatest among us...a servant.
All:	(*Somberly*) We get it.

THE END.

"DTR: DEFINE THE RELATIONSHIP"
BY EDDIE JAMES & TOMMY WOODARD WITH THE SKITIOTS

WHAT: As confusing as relationships can be, there usually comes a time when it's necessary to sit down together, share our feelings, and figure out where things are headed. When things get rough, it never hurts to have a good old DTR moment—one where you *Define The Relationship*. (Themes: feelings, understanding, communication, faith, needs)

WHO: Guy, Girl, Bill, Sally, Vickie, John, Eric, God

WHEN: Present day

WHY: Proverbs 3:5-6; Romans 5:8; 1 Corinthians 13:13

WEAR:
(COSTUMES AND PROPS)   Normal, everyday attire. This skit moves quickly, so it doesn't necessarily need props—in fact, props could weigh down the pace of the skit. Pantomime the different objects.

HOW: Be careful in the follow-through of pantomiming the different objects: opening the door, scanning groceries, and so on. If overdone (or, more likely, underdone), this could come across as overly cheesy. If done properly, the pantomiming can add significantly to the great scenes before you.

SCENE ONE: ***Guy*** *and* ***Girl*** *approach a restaurant, preparing for a date.*

Girl: I'm so excited we're going to my favorite restaurant! I love this place! Oh yeah, you said you had something you wanted to talk to me about?

Guy: Yeah, I did. Uh, before we go in…

Girl: You don't want to go in? Why not?

Guy: There were just some things I wanted to talk about out here, and I didn't want to make a big scene…

Girl:	Hold on—are you breaking up with me?
Guy:	No, I'm not breaking up with you. I just wanted us to have a DTR.
Girl:	A D-T-what?
Guy:	A DTR. You know—"Define The Relationship."
Girl:	What's there to define? I mean, we're dating, aren't we?
Guy:	(*Begins to ramble nervously*) I know, I just feel like there's so much more we could have. And there's so much about you that I don't know but that I want to know. And there's stuff you don't know about me and I want you to know it—and I just want to figure out where this thing is headed.
Girl:	I can tell you exactly where this is headed! Listen, I'm hungry. Let's go inside and get something to eat. I mean, I'm starving; you look like you're starving…
Guy:	Wait a minute—I look like I'm starving? Am I too skinny for you?
Girl:	That's not what I said!
Guy:	I'm not good enough for you, is that it? I'm just skin and bones?
Girl:	No, that's not what I said. I didn't say you were skinny. No, no, you're not skinny at all.
Guy:	So you think I'm fat?
Girl:	No, no, that's not what I—
Guy:	One minute you can't wait to get in the door of the restaurant, and the next you're telling me I need to lose weight? Wow! I guess I was right about us not knowing each other.
Girl:	What?
Guy:	Well, I had no idea that you thought I was too fat for you—and you apparently had no idea that I actually have feelings. I hope you enjoy your meal—alone!

Girl: What are you doing?

Guy: I just want you to know...I love you.

Girl: Uh...thanks...can we eat now?

SCENE TWO: *Grocery store checkout counter.* **Bill** *brings his groceries to* **Sally's** *counter as she says farewell to her previous customer.*

Sally: Thanks for shopping at Piggly Wiggly! Have a Piggly Wiggly day! Hey, Bill!

Bill: Hey, uh...(*reads nametag*) Sally.

Sally: Grocery shopping? (*Begins to scan* **Bill's** *items*)

Bill: Uh, yes, that's what people usually do at the grocery store.

Sally: (*Finds something unusual in cart*) Potpies instead of Hot Pockets, huh? What's going on?

Bill: I don't know, I was just in the mood for potpies, I guess.

Sally: But that's not what you got last week. That's just a little strange to me, but no big deal. (*Picks up another item*) Oh, two percent milk instead of skim? Are you okay?

Bill: Yeah...what are you talking about?

Sally: (*Acting hurt*) Nothing, it's just that you think you know someone, and then it turns out that you don't.

Bill: Is there something wrong?

Sally: Yes, there is. Bill, I think it's time for us to have a DTR.

Bill: A DTR? What's there to define? You're the checker at the grocery store!

Sally: I'm sorry, this line is closed. (*Pretends to close checkout line behind* **Bill**)

Bill: What are you doing? I just want to pay for my groceries and leave.

Sally:	You want to leave! Does that mean you're mad at me? Have I done something wrong? Because there are obviously things you aren't telling me. I mean, two percent? What's wrong, Bill? Talk to me. We can't work this thing out if you don't talk to me.
Bill:	I don't know why I need to explain myself!
Sally:	Because I am not a mind reader, Bill.
Bill:	I know. You're the checker at the grocery store!
Sally:	But things are changing between us, and I can't keep up. Oh, today it may be Hot Pockets to potpies, but the next thing you know, you'll want to change from orange juice to grapefruit juice. Then it's just a few steps from regular to decaf. Is that what you want to see happen, Bill? Is it?
Bill:	What? I just want to...
Sally:	I scan, and I scan, and I scan...
Bill:	What are you trying to say?
Sally:	I'm trying to say, "I love you!" (*Blows kiss to **Bill***)
Bill:	Thanks...I'm going to run for my life now. (*Hurriedly grabbing his groceries, **Bill** exits*)

*SCENE THREE: High-end beauty salon. Customer **Vickie** sits down in **John's** chair for a haircut.*

John:	All right, number 32, cut and shampoo? Vickie?
Vickie:	John! Hi, how are you?
John:	I'm doing great! Wow, it's been so long!
Vickie:	I know. Things have been so crazy lately, and I needed a trim, so I thought I'd just pop in and...
John:	(*Examining **Vickie's** hair*) Are these highlights?
Vickie:	Um...yeah.

John: They're good.

Vickie: (*Uneasily*) Thanks.

John: And what are these? Are these layers?

Vickie: A few.

John: Hmm, I don't remember putting layers in your hair. Um, Vickie, I think we need to have a DTR.

Vickie: What? No, there's nothing to talk about. I just came to my hairstylist to get things in shape.

John: I want you to answer me truthfully: Is there someone else?

Vickie: John, I can explain. I've been going to you for years, right? I don't know; I just wanted to see what else was out there. It didn't mean a thing, I promise!

John: So what, you couldn't call? You couldn't get some advice before you made some rash decision? Before you let some wacko crazy person cut your hair? You had no idea what you were getting yourself into!

Vickie: It's just a haircut, John. What's the worst that could happen?

John: Vickie, Vickie, Vickie—you are so naive. Whoever this guy was, he was teasing you.

Vickie: What?

John: I can look at your split ends and tell: He teased your hair.

Vickie: But John, it's not like that! I like you. I came back!

John: What's the point? What's to keep you from going to the next Toni and Guy that you see walking down the street?

Vickie: (*Offended*) Okay, I haven't been to Toni and Guy for years, and you know that! That's not fair! John, I came for a simple haircut...what are you doing?

John:	Vickie…I don't want to be just your rebound hairdresser. I want you to know that I love you.
Vickie:	Thanks. Are you okay to handle the scissors now?

SCENE FOUR: **Eric** *sitting in his room, praying.* **God** *joins him.*

God:	Eric, I think we need to have a DTR.
Eric:	I think that's a great idea, God. I mean, when I signed on to this relationship, I thought there was going to be a little more give-and-take.
God:	I'm sorry?
Eric:	I mean, don't get me wrong; I love this world you created for me to live in. And it's cool that Jesus was here and everything. But what have you done for me lately?
God:	Excuse me?
Eric:	Seriously, I go to church regularly; I tithe faithfully; I turn the other cheek; I do all that stuff—but my life is still so stressful! There's all this pressure to do what's right, to tell other people about you, to avoid temptation, yada, yada, yada. I mean, when's it gonna let up? When do I get to see the benefits of this relationship?
God:	Eric, I'm going to break some bad news to you. You don't get to define this relationship. I'm God, and you're not. But, I will never rip you off. I will never forget about you. I care about you so much that I want to see you grow—and when you're experiencing stress in your life, I'm helping you grow. I have great things planned for you, if you will persevere. Trust me, I know what I'm doing.
Eric:	Well, maybe if you gave me just a hint of where all this was headed, then…
God:	Then you wouldn't need to have faith in me. I've asked you to walk by faith, not by sight.
Eric:	It's just that I feel so out of control.

God: Good. You're not supposed to be in control. I am. Eric, I created everything that exists with just the words of my mouth. I put everything in order. I control nature and tell the oceans where to start and stop. I created gravity to make sure things don't fall off this planet as it flies around the sun at 67,000 miles per hour. All of this testifies that I'm not out of control. I see where you are, I know where you've been, and I know what's right around the corner. I have you in the palm of my hand, and I will not drop you.

Eric: So I'm just supposed to trust you.

God: Yes. It's called faith. Your faith in me helps define where you are in our relationship.

Eric: What are you trying to say to me, God?

God: I'm telling you that you can trust me. Eric, I love you.

Eric: Thanks. (*Pause*) I love you, too.

THE END.

"HERE COME THE BRIDES"

BY EDDIE JAMES & TOMMY WOODARD WITH GINNY LEE ELLIS & BRIAN CROPP

WHAT: This skit reveals how drastically the dating choices we make can affect our relationships in the future. (Themes: faithfulness, integrity, purity, marriage, promiscuity)

WHO: Emma, Doug, Minister, Bridesmaids, Groomsmen, Girl 1, Girl 2, Girl 3, Scott, Optional others as you see fit

WHERE: Wedding ceremony

WHEN: Present day

WHY: Proverbs 4:23; Song of Solomon 8:6; Romans 12:1-2

WEAR: Use whatever props and costumes you feel will help the audience connect
(COSTUMES AND PROPS)   with this skit. The "Wedding March" would be a great addition to play during the first part of the ceremony. Additional props: tuxedos, flowers, bridal gown, bridesmaids' dresses

HOW: This would be a great opportunity to utilize some less-experienced actors in the shorter or non-speaking parts to grow their confidence. Overall, the feel should be that of a realistic wedding.

Keep in mind: this is a major ensemble piece and will take ample rehearsal time.

---

*The skit starts as wedding music begins. The **Bridesmaids** and **Groomsmen** slowly enter and walk down the aisle. As the last pair enters, the bride, **Emma,** is seen. She slowly walks down the aisle and then to the altar looking at **Doug,** the groom. The **Minister** is standing at the front.*

Minister: Dearly beloved, we are gathered here today to celebrate the union of Emma Jane and Doug Lewis. We have spent our time watching these two during their courtship, and now we all have the privilege of seeing the product of their healthy relationship as they say their vows. They are beginning their walk in holy matrimony with the promise to love and cherish one another. (*Pause, looks at the happy couple*) The love from Emma's heart and the love from Doug's heart are joining together to form one—one heart that will continue to be united in love until death parts them.

*Slowly **Girl 1** makes her way down the aisle, stands by the groom, and links arms with him. **Doug** doesn't acknowledge her, and **Emma** looks confused.*

Minister: As we proceed with today's ceremony, Emma and Doug would like to take this moment to voice their love for one another. Doug, would you please begin?

Doug: Emma, I love you. It was love at first sight when my eyes fell upon you. I knew that there would be no one else who could make me feel the way you make me feel.

*As **Doug** is speaking, **Emma** is soothed, until **Girl 2** walks down the aisle and links arms with **Girl 1**. **Emma** is confused again.*

Doug: Since the very day that I proposed and you said yes, I knew it would be just us for the rest of our lives. Nothing can break us apart.

*On the word "apart," **Girl 3** walks down the aisle and links arms with **Girl 2**. **Emma's** stress increases.*

Girl 1: (*To **Girl 2***) That was so sweet.

Girl 2: I know. Doug was always so good with words.

Minister: Emma, it's your turn.

Emma: Doug, I…I…I can't do this.

Everyone in the wedding party reacts with shock.

Bridesmaid: Emma, are you all right?

Emma: No, I'm not all right.

Doug: What's wrong?

Emma: What's wrong? What's *wrong*? (*Indicating the chain of girls on **Doug's** arm*) That. That's what's wrong.

Doug: Sweetheart, let's…

Emma:	Don't "sweetheart" me! I've waited my whole life for this moment!
Doug:	Emma, calm down. We're getting married, aren't we?
Emma:	Married? How can we get married, Doug? Who are these women?
Doug:	(*Ignoring the other women*) Honey, these are women from my past—women I've been with—ex-girlfriends. I guess I could introduce you…
Emma:	Are you kidding? I don't want to meet them! How can you be clinging to the past when we are uniting our hearts for the future—as one?
Doug:	It's a little complicated. You see, I've already given pieces of my heart to them, so…
Emma:	(*Near tears*) What about me?
Doug:	I don't…
Emma:	What do I get?

Pause.

Girl 3:	(*To **Girl 2***) Let's see how he gets out of this one.
Doug:	You get everything that's left over.
Girl 3:	Wrong answer.
Emma:	Will they always be with us?
Doug:	I'm afraid so. I would've told you, but it's a little awkward. I mean, I don't want to spend the rest of my life with them, and I know they would say the same about me.
Girl 1:	He's right.
Girl 3:	You can have him.

*Pause, **Girls 1** and **3** look at **Girl 2.***

Girl 2:	What? I think I still love him.

Girls 1 and 3 roll their eyes at her.

Emma:	We never talked about this.
Doug:	Why should we? With these girls, I was just having some fun.
Emma:	Doug, this doesn't feel fun. This is our life we're talking about. What were you thinking? Now I'll see them whenever we…I'll wonder if you are thinking about them whenever we…
Doug:	This is why I didn't want to tell you. (*Takes a deep breath and tries a different tactic*) I won't think about them…I won't…I promise.
Girl 3:	I've heard that before.
Emma:	Is that what you told *them*? Was it?

Girls are nodding their heads in agreement.

Doug:	That's not fair, Emma.
Emma:	What's not fair is that this is our wedding, and I'm having to share it with…with…
Girl 1:	Lisa.
Girl 2:	Bridget.
Girl 3:	Tina.
Doug:	Are you telling me you don't have any skeletons in your closet? No one who could line up on your side?
Emma:	Do you see anyone?

Scott, sitting in the audience, stands up at this point.

Scott:	What about me, Emma? When were you going to tell your precious husband about me?

Emma:	Scott McLaughlin? You were my square-dance partner in fifth-grade P.E.!
Scott:	That's right! But we have a love connection that you can't deny.
Emma:	Scott, we never went out. I don't even think I've spoken to you since middle school.
Scott:	But I love you, Emma!
Emma:	Sit down, Scott. (**Scott** *sheepishly sits down*) Doug, do you see anyone? Anyone at all?
Doug:	No.
Emma:	Doug, from day one, you've known what I'm about. Even the times we got a little steamy, I'd tell you no. And I thought you respected me. But you didn't tell me about your past, your secrets. We should have talked about this stuff way before our wedding day. Maybe since you didn't bring it up I just assumed that you'd saved yourself. (*Pause*) You told me we were "on the same page," but I don't think we were even reading out of the same book. If my ex-boyfriends were here today and they all lined up on my side, I'd be able to look each one in the eyes without guilt or shame. You can't even *look* at the ghosts of your past, which makes me wonder what went on between you and them and how you must have treated them. We need more time, Doug. I need more time. To know the true you—warts…ghosts…all of it. (*Looks to the audience*) Sorry, everyone, this wedding won't be happening today.

Emma leaves crying, followed by a *Bridesmaid.*

THE END.

ALTERNATE ENDING: If you would rather end this skit with a funny moment, continue with the following dialogue after **Emma** *exits.*

Scott:	(*Standing up in the audience again*) Don't go, Emma. I'll marry you! I love you, Emma!
Girls 1, 2, 3:	Shut up, Scott!

THE END.

DRAMATIC READINGS

6.0

IN THE BEGINNING WAS THE WORD

At one time it was new and unique. Then it became old and boring. Now what once was lost has been found—the art of dramatic Scripture readings.

Do you remember the first time you saw a Scripture reading in church? You may have watched as several people stood there at the front of the sanctuary with folders in hand—just reading. Occasionally they would take turns—reading—words—in—a—sentence. Reading like the tick—tock—of—a—(*everybody together*) metronome. By the end of the reading you—were—totally—asleep. That is, unless your best friend was sitting next to you and you were both doing your best not to laugh out loud. Those readings always seemed like what churches would do if they couldn't pull off a real skit.

However, dramatic Scripture readings have made an impressive comeback, much like Lee Majors did when he came back to play *The Fall Guy*. (Now that was a million-dollar move!) The key to doing a good Scripture reading is found in looking at the "big picture." What are you trying to accomplish? How can you make it more interesting than just listening to people read? Are you using people who can read the passage in an engaging and entertaining way? After all, the Bible is the divine Word of God! It deserves the utmost respect if you want it to have the utmost impact on the listeners.

If you think you can simply choose a passage, pick some readers, and jump in without any practice, you're in for a surprise. That's a recipe for a crummy, boring performance. A successful reading involves the right passage, divided the right way, being read by the right people. Done effectively, a good Scripture reading can bring a passage alive like nothing else. Unless you can get James Earl Jones to read it!

SKIT TIPS

1. **FLEX YOUR CORDS.** It's a travesty when someone reads the Bible and puts other people to sleep. We've all experienced a time when a person killed the living Word by

reading it in a monotone voice. Utilize inflection in your voice. Realize that what you're reading is the greatest truth ever known. Don't overdo it, as though you're reading a children's story; simply make your reading as natural and energetic as possible.

2. **DON'T BE COLD.** If you try to do a "cold reading" in front of an audience, you'll get a cold reception. Although readings can be easier to put together than an actual skit, you still need to take the time to read through them several times in advance to get an idea of the appropriate tempo and flow of the piece. A few good rehearsals and read-throughs may even help develop more creative ideas for the readings. As you do those rehearsals, if you have sound and lighting technicians, have them sit in and watch. They may come up with some simple lighting or sound effects that could make your reading a home run.

3. **DON'T STOP, DON'T STOP THE MUSIC.** Some readings are very effective with nothing but silence behind them. However, using background music can give your reading more meaning and more emotion. Try to choose music that flows with the tempo of the reading. Also, an occasional Scripture reading can really be an incredible addition to your worship time. The idea is to have a seamless transition from worship music into the reading and right back into singing. What a powerful moment it would be if your musician(s) could flow from backing up your reading and straight into leading your group in worship.

4. **LEAVE THE CHEEZ WHIZ® AT HOME.** Of all the different types of dramatic presentations in this book, Scripture readings are the easiest to cheesify. Make sure your readers work hard to avoid the obvious cheese traps that lie waiting for them in the creative venue. For instance, no using a British accent. No moving the head like a beauty contestant reciting her plan to change the world. And as always, avoid—talking—at—a—tempo—like—a—metronome!

5. **THIS IS AN "ALL SKATE" IN VERSE DIRECTION.** If you're using presentation software (such as PowerPoint or MediaShout), then give the audience a chance to read with you. It will engage them more and help them relate to the reading if they're allowed to participate. Simply mark the Scripture you want them to recite in a way that will make it simple for them to follow along. The audience doesn't have to read all of the passage, just have them join in when it's appropriate between the actors' lines.

6. **NOTHING IS AS GOOD AS HOMEMADE BREAD.** We've given you some Scripture readings to get your feet wet, but we encourage you to start thinking of some passages you'd like to use in this form of communication. It's amazing to watch people react to something that's so simple. This form of theater is a great way to help people learn from and read the Bible—some for the first time, and some who haven't done so in a very long time.

"THE HOLINESS OF GOD"
BY EDDIE JAMES & TOMMY WOODARD

WHAT: A script in the traditional style about the holiness of God, this reading uses Scripture to paint an accurate picture of God's character. On the "all" parts, use PowerPoint or MediaShout if possible, or print up sheets with the Scripture on it, so the group can easily follow along. (Themes: holiness, God's character, heaven)

WHO: Reader, All

WHEN: Present day

WHY: Isaiah 44–46; Psalm 8:4; Revelation 21:1

WEAR: Music stands, folders for the Scripture readings
(COSTUMES AND PROPS)

HOW: While this style may be perceived as "old school," it's dynamic to hear and read God's Word when we're together as the body of Christ. Set this up properly, and there will be more excitement than boredom.

Reader: I am the Lord, who has made all things, who alone stretched out the heavens, who spread out the earth by myself, who foils the signs of false prophets and makes fools of diviners, who overthrows the learning of the wise and turns it into nonsense. I form the light and create the darkness. I bring prosperity and create disaster.

All: He is the Lord, and there is no other.

Reader: I, the Lord, speak the truth; I declare what is right. I am the first, and I am the last. My own hand laid the foundation of the earth, and my right hand spread out the heavens; when I summon them, they all stand up together. It is I who made the earth and created humanity upon it. I am the Lord, who exercises kindness, justice, and righteousness on earth, for in these I delight.

All: He is the Lord, our Holy One, Israel's Creator, our King.

Reader:	I make known the end from the beginning, from ancient times, what is to come. I say: My purpose will stand, and I will do all that I please. What I have said, that will I bring about; what I have planned, that will I do. Before me every knee will bow; by me every tongue will swear. They will say of me:
All:	In the Lord alone is righteousness and strength.
Reader:	I live in a high and holy place.
All:	But also with him who is contrite and lowly in spirit, to revive the spirit of the lowly and revive the heart of the contrite.
Reader:	I, even I, am the Lord, and apart from me there is no Savior. I have revealed and saved and proclaimed—I am not some foreign god among you. I am he, I am he who will sustain you. I have made you and I will carry you; I will sustain you and I will rescue you.
All:	He blots out our transgressions, for his own sake, and remembers our sins no more.
Reader:	Turn to me and be saved, all you ends of the earth, for I am God, and there is no other. I am the Lord, and that is my name. I will not give my glory to another, or my praise to idols. I am God, and there is no other; I am God, and there is none like me.
All:	What is man that you are mindful of him, the son of man that you care for him? For we all like sheep have gone astray, each of us to his own way. But we are all as an unclean thing, and all our righteousness is as filthy rags; and we all do fade as a leaf; and our iniquities, like the wind, have taken us away.
Reader:	I, the Lord, have called you in righteousness; I will take hold of your hand. I will keep you and make you to be a covenant for the people and a light for the Gentiles, to open the eyes that are blind, to free the captives from prison, and to release from the dungeon those who sit in darkness.
All:	But because of his great love for us, God, who is rich in mercy, made us alive with Christ even when we were dead in transgression—it is by grace we have been saved.
Reader:	But now this is what the Lord says—he who created you, O Jacob, he who formed you, O Israel: "Fear not for I have redeemed you; I have summoned you by name; you are mine."

All:	We are his. Now we are children of God.
Reader:	I will give them an undivided heart and put a new spirit in them; I will remove from them their heart of stone and give them a heart of flesh. Then they will follow my decrees and be careful to keep my laws. They will be my people, and I will be their God.
All:	We will be his people, and he will be our God.
Reader:	No longer will violence be heard in your land, nor ruin or destruction within your borders, but you will call your walls Salvation, and your gates Praise.
All:	We will be his people, and he will be our King.
Reader:	He who has ears, let him hear. Then I saw a new heaven and a new earth, for the first heaven and the first earth had passed away, and there was no longer any sea.
All:	I saw the Holy City, the New Jerusalem, coming down out of heaven from God, prepared as a bride beautifully dressed for her husband. And I heard a loud voice from the throne saying:
Reader:	Now the dwelling of God is with men, and he will live with them. They will be his people, and God himself will be with them and be their God.
All:	He will wipe every tear from our eyes. There will be no more death or mourning or crying or pain, for the old order of things has passed away. We will be his people, and he will be our King!
Reader:	And they cried out in a loud voice:
All:	Salvation belongs to our God, who sits on the throne, and to the Lamb.
Reader:	And all the angels were standing around the throne and around the elders and the four living creatures. They fell down on their faces before the throne and worshiped God, saying:
All:	Amen! Praise and glory and wisdom and thanks and honor and power and strength be to our God forever and ever. Amen!

THE END.

"THE LIFE OF CHRIST"

BY EDDIE JAMES & TOMMY WOODARD WITH J.R. VASSER

WHAT: Through different phases of Jesus' life, this responsive reading exemplifies the characteristics of an amazing Savior. (Themes: Jesus, Christmas, Easter, power of Christ)

WHO: Reader, All

WHEN: Present day

WHY: Luke 2:8-14; John 1:1-5, 14; Colossians 1:15-17; Philippians 2:6-11; Isaiah 53:4-7; Revelation 19:1, 4:6-8, 5:11-13

WEAR: Music stands, folders for the Scripture readings

(COSTUMES
AND PROPS)

HOW: The reading can start steady and build as if climbing stairs as you reach the end. Music in the background can bring it to another level for the audience.

Luke 2:8-14

Reader: That night some shepherds were in the fields outside the village, guarding their flocks of sheep. Suddenly, an angel of the Lord appeared among them, and the radiance of the Lord's glory surrounded them. They were terribly frightened, but the angel reassured them. "Don't be afraid!" he said. "I bring you good news of great joy for everyone!"

All: The Savior—yes, the Messiah, the Lord—has been born tonight in Bethlehem, the city of David!

Reader: Suddenly, the angel was joined by a vast host of other angels praising God:

All: "Glory to God in the highest heaven, and peace on earth to all whom God favors."

John 1:1-5, 14

Reader: In the beginning the Word already existed. He was with God, and he was God. He was in the beginning with God. He created everything there is. Nothing exists that he didn't make. Life itself was in him, and this life gives light to everyone. The light shines through the darkness, and the darkness can never extinguish it.

All: So the Word became human and lived here on earth among us. He was full of unfailing love and faithfulness. And we have seen his glory, the glory of the only Son of the Father.

Colossians 1:15-17

Reader: Christ is the visible image of the invisible God. He existed before God made anything at all and is supreme over all creation. Christ is the One through whom God created everything in heaven and earth. He made the things we can see and the things we can't see—kings, kingdoms, rulers, and authorities. Everything has been created through him and for him.

All: He existed before everything else began, and he holds all creation together.

Philippians 2:6-8

Reader: Though he was God, he did not demand and cling to his rights as God. He made himself nothing; he took the humble position of a slave and appeared in human form. And in human form he obediently humbled himself even further by dying a criminal's death on a cross.

Isaiah 53:4-7

Reader: Yet it was our weaknesses he carried; it was our sorrows that weighted him down. And we thought his troubles were a punishment from God for his own sins. But he was wounded and crushed for our sins. He was beaten that we might have peace. He was whipped, and we were healed.

All: All of us have strayed away like sheep. We have left God's paths to follow our own. Yet the Lord laid on him the guilt and sins of us all.

Philippians 2:9-11

Reader: Because of this, God raised him up to the heights of heaven and gave him a name that is above every other name, so that at the name of Jesus every knee will bow, in heaven and on earth and under the earth. Every tongue will confess that Jesus Christ is Lord, to the glory of God the Father.

Revelation 19:1

All: Hallelujah! Salvation is from our God. Glory and power belong to him alone.

Revelation 4:6-8

Reader: In front of the throne was a shiny sea of glass, sparkling like crystal. In the center and around the throne were four living beings, each covered with eyes, inside and out. Day after day and night after night they kept on saying,

All: "Holy, holy, holy is the Lord God Almighty—the One who always was, who is, and who is still to come."

Revelation 5:11-13

Reader: Then I looked again, and I heard the singing of thousands and millions of angels around the throne and the living beings and the elders. And they sang in a mighty chorus:

All: "The Lamb is worthy—the Lamb who was killed. He is worthy to receive power and riches and wisdom and strength and honor and glory and blessing."

Reader: And then I heard every creature in heaven and on earth and under the earth and in the sea. They also sang:

All: "Blessing and honor and glory and power belong to the One sitting on the throne and to the Lamb forever and ever."

THE END.

"ATTACKING JOB"

BY TOMMY WOODARD & EDDIE JAMES

WHAT: By reading Scripture, we see just how brutal and painful the verbal attacks of Job's friends were, and how faithful Job was to stand firm. (Themes: faith, trust in God, dedication, godly counsel)

WHO: Speaker, Job's Wife, Eliphaz, Bildad, Zophar, Elihu

WHEN: Biblical times

WHY: The book of Job

WEAR: Microphone on a stand at center stage, notebooks to put Scripture inside

(COSTUMES AND PROPS)

HOW: Pacing will be key in this reading. Adding characters to the voices you portray can make this Old Testament passage far more entertaining.

Speaker: "In the land of Uz there lived a man whose name was Job. This man was blameless and upright; he feared God and shunned evil. He had seven sons and three daughters, and he owned 7,000 sheep, 3,000 camels, 500 yoke of oxen and 500 donkeys, and had a large number of servants. He was the greatest man among all the people of the East." (Job 1:1-3)

One day, God was telling Satan how awesome Job was. Satan told God the only reason Job was this way was because God had blessed him so much. If Job were to lose everything he had, he'd fall apart and curse God. So God allowed Satan to take everything away from Job except for his own life.

First, Job lost all of his oxen. Second, his sheep. Third, his camels. Then he lost all of his servants; then, his children. Finally, he was with afflicted with "painful sores from the soles of his feet to the top of his head" (Job 2:7).

But Job never cursed God. He continued to be blameless and upright.

The first person to attack Job in his time of distress was his wife.

Wife enters and walks to microphone.

Wife: Are you still holding on to your integrity? Curse God and die!

Wife moves to stand at spot A; Eliphaz enters and walks to microphone.

Speaker: Job also had four friends who thought they knew what he needed to hear. The first was Eliphaz.

Eliphaz: Consider now: Who, being innocent, has ever perished? Where were the upright ever destroyed? As I have observed, those who plow evil and those who sow trouble reap it.

Eliphaz moves to spot B; Bildad enters and walks to microphone.

Speaker: Next was Bildad.

Bildad: But if you will look to God and plead with the Almighty, if you are pure and upright, even now he will rouse himself on your behalf and restore you to your rightful place.

Bildad moves to spot C; Zophar enters and walks to the microphone.

Speaker: Then came Zophar.

Zophar: If you put away the sin that is in your hand and allow no evil to dwell in your tent, then you will lift up your face without shame; you will stand firm and without fear.

Zophar moves to spot D; Elihu enters and walks to the microphone.

Speaker: And finally, Elihu.

Elihu: Oh, that Job might be tested to the utmost for answering like a wicked man! To his sin he adds rebellion; scornfully he claps his hands among us and multiplies his words against God.

Elihu moves to spot E.

Speaker: Can you imagine what it must have been like to hear all these things, over and over, day after day?

Each actor begins to say the next lines simultaneously, repeating the lines over and over, becoming louder.

Job's Wife: Curse God and die!

Eliphaz: Those who sow trouble reap it!

Bildad: If you are pure and upright, he will restore you!

Zophar: Put away the sin that is in your hand!

Elihu: You're a sinner and a rebel!

*Actors continue to repeat their lines as **Speaker** begins to speak.*

Speaker: So what did Job do in the face of these attacks? Did he curse the God he loved? Did he confess to sin he hadn't committed? (*Actors fall silent*) No, he didn't. Job, God's servant, was faithful.

THE END.

STAGE SETUP:

C

D   B

E   Speaker

A

Audience • Audience • Audience • Audience • Audience
Audience • Audience • Audience • Audience • Audience • Audience
Audience • Audience • Audience • Audience • Audience
Audience • Audience • Audience • Audience • Audience • Audience
Audience • Audience • Audience • Audience • Audience
Audience • Audience • Audience • Audience • Audience • Audience

"YOU WASH MY FEET, LORD?"

BY EDDIE JAMES & TOMMY WOODARD

WHAT: As the time approaches for Jesus to accomplish his purpose on earth, he gathers his disciples to prepare them in the last way they would expect. (Themes: servanthood, humility, Easter, the Lord's Supper)

WHO: Narrator, Peter, Jesus

WHEN: Biblical times

WHY: John 13:1-17

WEAR: Large bowl, apron, pitcher, towel

(COSTUMES
AND PROPS)

HOW: On its own, this is a creative way to share this passage from John 13. However, some more creative ideas would include:

1. Adding music behind it. Be creative; don't use the usual "background" music. Choose something that will reach your audience and move them.

2. Having two people actually perform a foot washing in front of your readers while they are reading. Play this down if you do it. Be simple.

Narrator: Just before the Passover Feast, Jesus knew that the time had come for him to leave this world and go to the Father. Having loved his dear companions, he continued to love them right to the end. It was suppertime. The devil by now had Judas, son of Simon the Iscariot, firmly in his grip, all set for the betrayal.

Jesus knew the Father had put him in complete charge of everything—that he came from God and was on his way back to God. So he got up from the supper table, set aside his robe, and put on an apron. Then he poured water into a basin and began to wash the feet of the disciples, drying them with his apron. When he got to Simon Peter, Peter said…

Peter:	Master, you wash *my* feet?
Narrator:	Jesus answered…
Jesus:	You don't understand what I'm doing now, but it will become clear to you later.
Narrator:	Peter persisted…
Peter:	You're not going to wash my feet—ever!
Narrator:	Jesus said…
Jesus:	If I don't wash you, you can't be part of what I'm doing.
Peter:	Master!
Narrator:	…said Peter…
Peter:	Not only my feet, then! Wash my hands! Wash my head!
Narrator:	Jesus said…
Jesus:	If you've had a bath in the morning, you only need your feet washed now and you're clean from head to toe. My concern, you understand, is holiness, not hygiene. So now you're clean. But not every one of you.
Narrator:	He knew who was betraying him. That's why he said, "Not every one of you." After he had finished washing their feet, he took his robe, put it back on, and went back to his place at the table. Then he said…
Jesus:	Do you understand what I have done to you? You address me as "Teacher" and "Master," and rightly so. That is what I am. So if I, the Master and Teacher, washed your feet, you must now wash each other's feet. I've laid down a pattern for you. What I've done, you do. I'm only pointing out the obvious—a servant is not ranked above his master; an employee doesn't give orders to the employer. If you understand what I'm telling you, act like it—and live a blessed life.

THE END.

"THE MEANING OF LOVE"

BY EDDIE JAMES & TOMMY WOODARD WITH CHARISSA FISHBECK

WHAT: These days, there is no word more misinterpreted than the word "love." This responsive reading is a very specific explanation of what love really is, and what it isn't. (Themes: love, sacrifice, faith, gift)

WHO: Reader 1, Reader 2, Reader 3

WHEN: Present day

WHY: Mark 12:30; Romans 5:8; 1 Corinthians 13; 1 John 4:8

WEAR: None

(COSTUMES AND PROPS)

HOW: This is a bit of a hybrid, in that the readers in this section actually interact with one another. You can begin as a dramatic reading and morph into some movement when they begin to interact. Or you may choose to keep them all in a line facing the audience and not look at each other even when their dialogue suggests interaction. Both can be done in powerful ways.

---

1 Corinthians 13:1-3

Reader 1: If I speak with the tongues of men and of angels, but have not love, I have become a noisy gong or a clanging cymbal.

Reader 2: If I have the gift of prophecy and know all mysteries and all knowledge, and if I have all faith, so as to remove mountains, but do not have love, I am nothing.

Reader 3: And if I give all my possessions to the poor, and if I surrender my body to be burned, but do not have love, it profits me nothing.

1 John 4:8

Reader 1:   The one who does not love does not know God, because God is love.

1 Corinthians 13:4-5

Reader 2:   Love is patient, love is kind and is not jealous, love does not brag and is not arrogant. God is love.

Reader 3:   Love does not act unbecomingly, it does not seek its own, it is not provoked, it does not take into account a wrong suffered. God is love.

Romans 5:8

Reader 1:   And God demonstrates his own love for us in this: While we were still sinners, Christ died for us.

1 Corinthians 13:6-8

Reader 2:   Love does not rejoice in unrighteousness, but rejoices with the truth.

Reader 3:   Love bears all things, believes all things, hopes all things, and endures all things. Love never fails.

Reader 1:   Okay, so we can read that passage, take the word "love" and replace it with "God," and we can find out exactly what God is like. I wonder what would happen if I put my own name there? "(**Reader** says actual name) is patient"—whoops, struck out already.

Reader 2:   Let me try! Okay, "(Name) is kind," yeah, sometimes, "and is not jealous," well, most of the time, "(name) does not brag," ouch, "and is not arrogant." Darn, this is tough! (To **Reader 3**) Your turn!

Reader 3:   "(Name) does not act unbecomingly"—wait, what does that mean, anyway?

Reader 1:   Let's just say that most of your actions at camp last summer could be considered "unbecoming."

Reader 3:	Oh, I had forgotten about that. Did (*name of student in youth group*) ever get all that peanut butter out of his hair? Never mind, let's go on to the next one. "(*Name*) does not seek its own, is not provoked, and does not take into account a wrong suffered." I bet my mom and dad would disagree.
Reader 1:	Yeah, mine, too. Along with pretty much all of my friends. Let's see what else there is…"(*Name*) does not rejoice in unrighteousness, but rejoices with the truth." Can I fit my name in this passage *anywhere*? *"(Name*) bears all things, believes all things, hopes all things, and endures all things. (*Name*) never fails." (*Pause*) Wow. Not only did I strike out, I think I've been kicked off the team and sent home.
Reader 2:	That's okay, we all have. But the good news is, God knew when this was written that we'd fall short sometimes. Nothing we've done surprises God a bit.
Reader 3:	So is there anything we can do to show God our love?
Reader 2:	Actually, there is. Look at what Jesus said in Mark 12:30 — "the first and greatest commandment."
Together:	Love the Lord your God with all your heart, and with all your soul, and with all your mind, and with all your strength.
Reader 1:	Now that, I can do.

THE END.